"I have read a lot of books about anxiety, and I ⟨...⟩ that *What Happened to Make You Anxious?* is the ⟨...⟩ that I couldn't put down. Jaime explains the many realities of anxiety plus what you can do about it in a relatable, interesting, and applicable way. If you struggle with anxiety, don't skip this one."

—**Elizabeth Earnshaw, LMFT**, author of *I Want This to Work*,
clinical fellow of the AAMFT, creator of @lizlistens on
Instagram, and cofounder of A Better Life Therapy

"*What Happened to Make You Anxious* by Jaime Castillo is truly an incredible resource for folks struggling with anxiety and underlying little 't' traumas! This book will help you to change your relationship to anxiety and live life according to your true values. Jaime helps you to explore not just your anxiety symptoms, but also the underlying function of your anxiety. I HIGHLY recommend this book to anyone who is feeling consumed by their anxiety and looking to improve their relationship with it!"

—**Jennifer Rollin, LCSW-C**, therapist, founder of
The Eating Disorder Center, and coauthor of *The Inside
Scoop on Eating Disorder Recovery*

"In a world where we are more anxious than ever, *What Happened to Make You Anxious?* is the smart and compassionate book we all need right now. In this warm and supportive guide, readers learn science-backed tools so that they can stop fighting their anxiety (and themselves) and start healing. This book is going to help so many!"

—**Amanda E. White, LPC**, founder of @therapyforwomen,
and author of *Not Drinking Tonight*

"If you've ever asked yourself, 'Why am I so anxious?,' this is the book that will finally give you a clear answer. Jaime's compassionate tone and easy-to-use strategies are guaranteed to help you understand, manage, and use your anxiety to help you in powerful ways."

—**Whitney Goodman, LMFT**, licensed psychotherapist, and author of *Toxic Positivity*

"This is a useful guide in helping readers approach their anxiety from a place of curiosity and understanding. Jaime offers direct and succinct tools that promote action and self-reflection. This is a must-read for the person who is ready to put the shame and self-criticism to the side and take steps to transform their relationship with anxiety!"

—**Alyssa Mancao, LCSW**, licensed clinical social worker; writer; and owner of Alyssa Marie Wellness Inc. located in Los Angeles, CA

"*What Happened to Make You Anxious* is more than a book; it is an insightful, practical guide—full of tools and resources for people who struggle not just with anxiety, but with finding ways to respond to their fears, doubts, and feelings of overwhelm in a manageable way. Jaime Castillo's work is beautifully written and full of professional wisdom. I highly recommend this read!"

—**Minaa B., LMSW**, writer, speaker, and therapist

"This book is fantastic, vulnerable, relatable, and versatile! It aims to help you understand the origins of anxiety, establish a relationship with worry, and cultivate connection with them to honor their purpose—as they serve as messengers. The activities within the book are creative and to the point. Jaime's beautiful and authentic anecdotes make you feel like you are chatting with a friend who really gets you."

—**Kelly O'Horo, LPC**, approved consultant, and founder of Infinite Healing and Wellness, an EMDR Center for Excellence; and contributing author of *Is Therapy Right for Me?*

What happened to make you anxious?

how to uncover
the little "t" traumas that drive
your anxiety, worry & fear

JAIME CASTILLO, LCSW

New Harbinger Publications, Inc.

Publisher's Note

Distributed in Canada by Raincoast Books

NEW HARBINGER PUBLICATIONS is a registered trademark of New Harbinger Publications, Inc.

Copyright © 2022 by Jaime Castillo
New Harbinger Publications, Inc.
5674 Shattuck Avenue
Oakland, CA 94609
www.newharbinger.com

Cover design by Amy Daniel; Acquired by Georgia Kolias; Edited by Krist Hein

Library of Congress Cataloging-in-Publication Data

Names: Castillo, Jaime (Psychologist) author.
Title: What happened to make you anxious? : how to uncover the little "t" traumas that drive your anxiety, worry, and fear / Jaime Castillo.
Description: Oakland, CA : New Harbinger Publications, 2022. | Includes bibliographical references.
Identifiers: LCCN 2022000692 | ISBN 9781684038756 (trade paperback)
Subjects: LCSH: Anxiety. | Fear. | Acceptance and commitment therapy.
Classification: LCC BF575.A6 C376 2022 | DDC 152.4/6--dc23/eng/20220125
LC record available at https://lccn.loc.gov/2022000692

Printed in the United States of America

24   23   22

10   9   8   7   6   5   4   3   2   1   First Printing

To Lance, whose love has given me courage.

contents

acknowledgments

To my husband, Lance, who has shown me unwavering love, support, and encouragement. To my parents, who taught me I can do anything I put my mind to, and to repeat the phrase *I think I can* when doing something hard (that came in handy several times while writing this book). To my brothers, whom I have looked up to and admired for forever; you are my heart. To my best friend, Chelsea, who convinced me that my voice was worthy of being heard. To my mentor, Sarah, who showed me the way as a budding therapist. To the Find Your Shine Therapy team, who bring me joy and inspiration every day. To my clients, who have trusted me with their stories. Thank you is not enough.

introduction

What if I told you that the way we have been taught to manage anxiety has actually made it worse? If our efforts to outrun or extinguish anxiety have actually fanned its flames? Anxiety is a necessary and adaptive human emotion that communicates important messages to us. It helps us to avoid danger and live a life in accordance with our values. So why does it cause so many problems in our lives? If anxiety is meant to be helpful, how is it that forty million people in the United States suffer from a clinical anxiety disorder?

Anxiety itself is not actually the culprit for the problems it seems to cause. Rather, our response to anxiety makes all the difference in how problematic it becomes. What we do when anxiety arises is a determining factor in whether we experience it as an occasional, helpful nudge toward our values or an unshakable force that robs us of life's pleasures.

Most of us have been conditioned to avoid anxiety whenever we notice its nudges. But because anxiety is actually there as an adaptive force to help keep us alive and well, it feels like the stakes are desperately high. Anxiety has a message that it will go to great lengths to deliver. When it's silenced, it raises its voice. When it's ignored, it tries another way to get our attention. It refuses to be outrun. It remains under the surface, waiting to be acknowledged. And it will be acknowledged at any cost to us.

If you have been at war with your anxiety for some time, it has likely started to cause problems in your work, social life, and/or intimate relationships. Anxiety is not just unpleasant to experience in the moment; over time, it can rob you of your sense of safety, connection, and overall well-being.

But there's another way. You don't have to be at odds with your anxiety any longer. When you can lean into your anxiety, understand the message it's trying to deliver and what is keeping it stuck, and then come to a mutual agreement about how to best solve the problem it is interpreting and insisting that you do something about, you find freedom.

I am going to show you exactly how to do this. Step by step, I will guide you through the process of turning toward your anxiety, allowing it to show you what it fears and where that fear originated, and then together uncovering and revisiting the past wounds that are the source of your anxiety. You will learn to befriend your anxiety rather than detaching from it and in so doing, detaching from yourself. This process will change your relationship to anxiety forever and allow you to start to live a more values-driven life.

I know this is possible for a couple of reasons. As a licensed therapist who specializes in treating anxiety, I have had the honor of guiding hundreds of people with anxiety through this journey to freedom. As a human with anxiety, I have walked through the process of uncovering my own unresolved past wounds that continued to fuel and strengthen my anxiety throughout my life. In the process, I was able to see my anxiety transform from a weekly anticipated and dreaded experience to an important insider with helpful information to share.

This book is informed by various behavioral theories and evidence-based therapeutic modalities, including the adaptive information processing (AIP) model, which informs eye movement desensitization and reprocessing (EMDR) therapy, internal family systems (IFS) therapy, and acceptance and commitment therapy (ACT). In this book I will use the most helpful and effective techniques from these interventions, combined with my years of experience in working with people on anxiety recovery, to guide you along this path to healing. There are also online free tools—audio files of the visualization exercises—available for download at the website for this book: http://www.newharbinger.com/48756. (See the very back of this book for more details.)

Most of us who live with anxiety have unresolved past wounds that either caused or contribute to it. However, anxiety can have many other causes. I recommend that you have medical causes of anxiety ruled out prior to engaging in this therapeutic work. Conditions like thyroid dysfunction, respiratory disorders, gastrointestinal problems, and the side effects of certain medications have been linked to anxiety. If you have an underlying medical condition that causes anxiety, it doesn't mean that this book is not appropriate for you; it just means you should have the medical issue treated first.

Anxiety occurs disproportionately in members of marginalized groups, likely a result of the effects of systemic oppression and stigma. Many studies have found associations between discrimination and anxiety, as well as other mental health conditions. The very real threats to safety that exist for members of oppressed groups cannot be overlooked. If you are a member of a marginalized group experiencing anxiety caused by discrimination, please note that it will not be possible to completely alleviate anxiety until systemic change occurs and the world becomes a safer place for you to be. That said, this book will be helpful for changing your relationship to your anxiety and for healing anxiety caused by past unresolved wounds, regardless of the type of wound.

Any threat to basic safety and/or survival is likely to cause anxiety for good reason. For example, most every one of us has experienced some level of anxiety related to the COVID-19 pandemic, which threatens our basic needs for safety and survival. If your basic needs are threatened by other issues—such as poverty, violence, food scarcity, or lack of access to health care—it may not be necessary to go searching for past unresolved wounds that are contributing to your anxiety, because your anxiety about these issues is clear, valid, and warranted.

In the chapters that follow, I'll help you distinguish between anxiety that fits the facts of the situation you're in, and anxiety that doesn't. We'll do therapeutic work together on the latter.

This book is not therapy, however. It is missing the most fundamental component of the therapeutic process: the relationship between client and therapist. It is also not meant to be a substitute for therapy. If you have been diagnosed with a mental health condition such as complex post-traumatic stress disorder (C-PTSD), a dissociative disorder, or obsessive-compulsive disorder (OCD) or are experiencing an active substance use or eating disorder, it is likely that this book will not provide the level of support you need.

The goal of this book is not to just help you manage symptoms of anxiety. It is more than breathing techniques and grounding skills. It is designed to take you on a journey into your past to explore where anxiety is "stuck," which will help you uncover why it is misfiring now. It is designed to get to the root of the problem so you can experience long-lasting change rather than continually searching for another method of coping with it. It will make the difference between avoiding anxiety and the parts of your life that come with it, and living fully.

CHAPTER 1

understanding anxiety

For most of my adult life I've lived with a fear of appearing ignorant, ill-prepared, inexperienced, unqualified—or to use that childhood insult, *dumb*—in front of respectable people. This fear manifested as an anxiety that accompanied me through my young adulthood and the beginnings of my professional life. As a budding therapist, I knew it made sense to experience *some* doubt or insecurity, but this anxiety was disproportionate. It sometimes felt almost disabling.

I can remember sitting in meetings at my first professional internship, surrounded by people much more experienced than I was, physically shaking when I knew it was almost my turn to present a client case. There was nothing that felt more threatening to me in those moments than the possibility of saying something stupid and discovering that I didn't have what it took to be a good therapist. I was terrified to show vulnerability in other ways; for example, I strategically neglected to tell anyone when my licensing exam was scheduled. If I failed, I couldn't tolerate the prospect of having to disclose that to my colleagues. In my mind, this would have revealed to them that I was actually not as smart and respectable as they might have thought. At that point in my life, this felt worse than death.

The thing is, my anxiety had very little basis in reality. Not only was I qualified to be at the table, but at the agency where I interned, my supervisors, mentors, and even my fellow interns genuinely embodied a culture of support, compassion, and the encouragement of growth. I had never been publicly shamed or made to feel stupid. So in fact, it was irrational to be thinking I would reveal myself as an imposter who didn't actually deserve to be there if I said the wrong thing. But to my anxiety, none of that really mattered. It was convinced that I was in danger, and it put my nervous system on high alert.

As you can imagine, my anxiety felt really uncomfortable to experience. So naturally I did what I could to avoid or suppress it. That's what we do as humans, right? We try to avoid pain, and when we can't, we try to ease it. This includes emotional pain. When I was trembling inside, I would do anything I could think of to make it stop: taking sips of ice water, naming things around the room I could see, and even using my newly minted cognitive behavioral therapy (CBT) skill of challenging my own thinking. While these tools helped some, the biggest relief came when the meeting was over. It was as if my nervous system exclaimed *Crisis averted!* and finally backed down just enough to allow me to take a full, deep breath. The relief I felt would stick around until the next weekly meeting was held. It became a predictable and seemingly unending cycle of anxiety and relief.

When Anxiety Doesn't Make Sense

Anxiety—the strong, persistent fear or apprehension that something bad is going to happen—doesn't need to make sense to be real. Often, anxiety does fit with the facts of the situation that prompts it—it's rational. With this type of anxiety, anyone might look at the situation and think, *I would feel anxious about that*. For example, if you lose your job and experience anxiety about how you are going to pay your bills, your anxiety fits the facts of what's happened. In this case, anxiety may actually be useful, because it may prompt you to engage in a job search and get creative about scaling back expenses. While the experience may be stressful, once you obtain a new job and can pay your bills, it's likely your anxiety will naturally reduce. Other examples of anxiety that fit the facts of the situation might relate to an important presentation or exam, a newly diagnosed medical condition, a first date, and so on.

Another kind of anxiety, the kind that we'll be working with in the chapters that follow, is the kind that doesn't fit the facts of the situation. It is irrational, sometimes distressingly so. For example:

- Feeling panic all of a sudden just before you meet up with friends whom you adore

- Feeling fear after having a random thought that your partner is pulling away from the relationship

- Having a rather calm and worry-free day and then starting to have anxiety because you *don't* currently have anxiety and don't want to be caught off guard

This type of anxiety can add layers of frustration and confusion to a situation. It can feel unpredictable. It may even leave you dumbfounded. With this type of anxiety, it's hard to imagine someone else looking at your situation with compassion, saying "I'd feel anxious about that too." If you communicate this type of anxiety, it may get the opposite of compassion: invalidation. You might hear things like "Just stop worrying about that," "Let it go," or (my personal favorite) "Chill out!"

You probably *want* to be able to stop worrying, let it go, chill out, and get on with your life. But when your anxiety feels irrational and unsolvable, you may feel like your only option is to ignore it, or detach from it, or numb it. After all, you have places to go, people to see, relationships to foster and maintain. And there's no way around it: anxiety gets in the way of all of these.

As if your desire to live without the discomfort of anxiety wasn't enough, your efforts to avoid anxiety may be further encouraged and reinforced by society in a number of ways. Our news and social media feeds have a hundred ways every day to remind us that our anxiety makes us unlikable. We are made to feel that we're doing something wrong when we live with anxiety and are simultaneously exposed over and over to perfectly curated Instagram feeds and people who appear to have it all together. The cultural pressure to measure up to our peers gives us even more incentive to suppress our signs of anxiety.

It makes good sense to want to get rid of our anxiety. It's incredibly uncomfortable to live with that feeling in the pit of your stomach or that can't-seem-to-get-a-full-breath sensation that anxiety often brings. It makes us feel out of control and helpless. And society says we won't fare very well as a partner, employee, or friend if our anxiety isn't well managed. The result? Most of us don't need convincing that we should want to reduce our anxiety.

Many people have tried everything under the sun to stop their anxiety from happening. People actually die from desperate attempts to control anxiety, such as numbing it with substances or other self-harming behaviors. Attempts to block, avoid, or numb anxiety might create some relief in the short term. But they often lead to dire consequences over time—at a minimum, a reinforcement and perpetuation of anxiety, and at worst, your life.

But what if there were another way to approach our anxiety?

Anxiety Can Be a Friend

When anxiety fits the facts of the situation you're in (that is, it's rational), there is nothing you need to do other than learn and use some basic anxiety-management techniques to cope the best you can in the moment. Then, if possible, problem solve the situation so that you can reduce its real dangers or discomforts. But if you frequently experience the kind of anxiety that doesn't fit the facts, or if you're not sure whether it does, or if anxiety seems to be causing problems in your life, this book is for you.

First, you will learn tools for temporarily calming anxiety because, let's be honest, talking about anxiety probably gives you anxiety. I want to make sure you're as equipped as possible to manage the emotions that might bubble to the surface as you start to do this work.

Most people who live with anxiety devote a great deal of energy to trying to suppress rather than understand it. This makes sense, in a way. When we're committed to putting out a fire and using all of our resources to do so, we can't simultaneously get to know why the fire started in the first place. As long as we are actively suppressing anxiety, our ability to understand it fully will be compromised. For that reason, I recommend choosing to engage with this text at times when your anxiety feels relatively managed, perhaps a 5 out of 10 or lower. The self-regulating tools will help you get there.

Next, you'll learn the role of avoidance in increasing and perpetuating anxiety and the need for moving toward rather than away from it to find true healing. You'll be guided through exercises designed to give you a better understanding of your unique anxiety how it manifests currently and where it all started. Everyone's anxiety is personal to them, and it's important to spend some time learning what yours is like. This makes it easier to see and to remember that *your anxiety* is not the same thing as *you*.

Once you're able to accept your anxiety as an entity separate from yourself, it becomes something you can be curious about and have a relationship with. You'll become able to repair your relationship with anxiety, seeing it in its true light as a protective part of yourself that wants the same things for you as *you* want for you. You'll learn to work *with* your anxiety rather than fighting against it and will be given opportunities for healing old wounds that are causing your brain to register threats that don't actually exist.

Finally, you'll establish a pact with your anxiety that will honor its purpose and function, while giving you enough space and distance from it that you will be able to live a meaningful, fulfilled, value-driven life that is no longer hijacked by fear.

REFLECTION: Your Coping Behaviors—A Journal Exercise

What efforts do you make to stop anxiety? Give this some reflection, and in your journal, write some of the tactics you regularly rely on. Maybe you avoid certain people or places. Maybe you have a glass of wine at the end of the day. Maybe you go for a run. Coping behaviors aren't always bad, but it's important to be able to get to know them and recognize them in real time for what they are: efforts to stop anxiety.

I know this process of befriending your own anxiety is possible, because I've done it myself. In the years since I was an intern trembling before speaking at my weekly staff meetings, I have learned and applied the skills I will teach you in the chapters that follow. I have transformed my relationship with my own anxiety, and I have helped hundreds of my clients do the same.

The Brain's Threat Meter

In my professional work as a therapist, as I continued gathering training and experience I started to better understand how and why the cycle of anxiety starts and perpetuates. When we live with anxiety, our threat meter becomes hijacked and causes us to feel the same level of threat—for example, in a professional meeting—as we would if we were out in the wild and saw a mountain lion approaching us. When the part of our brain that is designed to perceive and respond to threats is activated, it compromises the other part of our brain—the one designed to help us think logically, problem solve, and rationalize.

From an evolutionary perspective this is actually very useful, because if we encounter a lion in the wild we need to be able to act fast rather than pull out a piece of scratch paper and start listing our options in order of likelihood to help us survive. However, this mechanism creates challenges when our brain is perceiving a threat that doesn't actually exist (or exists on a *much* smaller, less threatening scale than we're perceiving). We need to be able to problem solve and rationalize, but the part of our brain that helps us do that isn't functioning well. This is why, when we're struggling with anxiety, advice from well-intentioned people like "Just stop worrying" or "Think happy thoughts!" feels invalidating. We would gladly do those things if we could, but our brain thinks we're about to be a lion's meal, so it's a little averse to putting that on the back burner and thinking about cute puppies instead. It's this same mechanism that makes efforts to reason with our anxiety feel futile.

When Anxiety Generalizes

Further complicating matters, the part of our brain that perceives threats isn't always discerning about what *part* of the experience was threatening. When a threat happens, our survival brain casts a really wide net. That's why if you are walking in a park on a rainy summer day and a tree you're passing is struck by lightning, your brain will register not only that lightning is dangerous, but perhaps also that rain, summer days, and that particular park are dangerous too. You may have a hard time revisiting that park after that experience, even though your logic would tell you that the park itself is not dangerous. Similarly, you may find it difficult to walk outside on rainy summer days, even if you know there is almost no likelihood that you would ever experience a close lightning strike again. This tendency to draw causation isn't limited to actual dangerous events, but also rings true for *perceived* danger, like the professional meetings I've described. For example, it would not have been surprising if my brain started to associate that particular meeting room with danger, causing anxiety when I was in that room even if for a completely different occasion.

REFLECTION: Your Threat Meter—A Journal Exercise

In what ways has your own anxiety generalized to things outside of the actual threat? Perhaps you had an anxiety attack in a certain location, and now you find that location provokes anxiety despite there being no real threat associated with it. Maybe your anxiety started in a social context but has become generalized over time to health anxiety, anxiety while driving, or some other unrelated form of anxiety. If you have a hard time linking your anxiety back to an actual threat, that's okay. While it may not be obvious now, my hope is that in doing this work, you will begin to get a clear picture of both the root of your anxiety and the ways it's generalized.

Just as our brains try to make sense of threats, they like to understand safety too. In the story I told at the beginning of this chapter, I mentioned that when a staff meeting was over, I felt instant relief. Our brains have a tendency to interpret that as *I felt relief* because *I got out of that meeting.* This reinforces the idea that meetings are dangerous and is likely to increase my anxiety the next time I'm in the meeting. It's as if our survival brain says to us, *See, I knew that meeting was life threatening. That's why you felt so much calmer when it ended. Best to avoid those meetings altogether going forward.* This is accurate when we experience anxiety that fits the facts, like if we were to encounter a lion in the wild. Once we escape the lion, it makes sense that our anxiety would lessen and we would take from that experience the message that we should avoid lions in the future. However, it doesn't make sense in the context of meetings.

So how do you break this cycle? The first step in this work is to better understand why the anxiety is there in the first place. After all, we can't change it if we don't know why it exists to begin with. Sometimes it's obvious, as in the lightning strike example. If we experience a close lightning strike in a park and subsequently experience fear of lightning and parks, we don't have to do a ton of investigative work to get to the bottom of why that's happening. Other times, though, there isn't such a clear and obvious cause, like when I experienced anxiety in my professional meetings. That's why it was so frustrating—I knew it was irrational and couldn't pinpoint why it was happening.

Anxiety as a Messenger

What I learned was that rather than trying to problem solve anxiety, rationalize myself out of it, or extinguish it, I needed to treat anxiety as a messenger that had important information for me about danger. It was working to protect me, even though its efforts were actually counterproductive. Once I shifted out of attempting to solve it and got curious about what it actually wanted from me, that is when healing happened.

Think of anxiety as a four-year-old child who randomly starts throwing a temper tantrum, screaming and flailing about. Imagine saying "Johnnie, it makes no sense that you're crying right now. This is ridiculous. Would you stop it?" If you have spent any amount of time around four-year-olds, you know what outcome this rationalizing approach would lead to: Johnnie is going to cry harder until his needs are met. It would be more effective to get down to his eye level with Johnnie and say, "What is it? Tell me. I'm here and I'm listening."

Anxiety wants the same thing from us. It's trying to tell us something, and as long as we try to rationalize or push it away, it's going to escalate, until we can sit with it and say, *What is it, anxiety? Show me.* Once you can change your relationship with anxiety in this way, you will start to notice a decrease in tension. Your anxiety will finally start to feel heard—because it is actually *being* heard.

And the communication goes both ways. It wasn't until I was at a professional training a couple of years ago that I finally opened up to my anxiety about feeling dumb. I was working in a professional dyad with a colleague, and my fear of sounding dumb came up in whatever we were discussing. My partner said, "Why don't you just close your eyes and explore that a bit?" She asked me to connect to the part of my body that felt anxious. It showed up immediately—it felt like the shape and weight of a ten-pound dumbbell sitting on my chest. She asked me to notice how I felt about it. Annoyed. Unwelcoming. She encouraged me to just notice it rather than try to push it away.

I sat there with my eyes closed, wondering *How much longer until this training is over?* Hadn't I just told her this anxiety was unwelcome? I didn't exactly want to sit with it, especially in the middle of a professional training. What if it got bigger or more powerful? What if it completely overtook me? I voiced these concerns, and she clearly had been paying attention to the training material, because she struck the perfect balance of validating my fears and encouraging me to continue this exercise despite them.

After some time, I agreed to sit with my anxiety without trying to detach from it. With the help of her prompts, I asked it what it feared. I listened for the answer. It told me it didn't want me to sound dumb or else I would be the laughingstock of whatever group I was in. Although I wasn't totally on board with its role yet, I was able to acknowledge that we shared a common goal. I didn't want that either. Actually, the thought of that terrified me. Over the next couple of days, my colleague continued to lead me through this inner work, and as she did, I started gleaning more and more important insights, which led to substantial mental shifts.

As you navigate this work, you too will gain a better understanding of how your anxiety is trying to help you. You will learn that you and your anxiety share a common goal for yourself but likely have different ideas about how best to achieve that goal.

Giving Anxiety a Voice

When I began this work, it was as if for the first time ever I paused on my fierce ascent up the mountain of life. In my peripheral vision I saw my friend anxiety flailing its arms and silently shouting in a desperate attempt to get my attention. I said, *Oh hi there. You must be trying to help me.* Just this step alone allowed my anxiety to breathe a huge sigh of relief. I had finally acknowledged it rather than trying to distance myself from it and power through. I noticed my anxiety already easing up. It was

the equivalent of sitting down on the floor with a completely dysregulated four-year-old.

This felt like a giant leap in my own healing journey, but as I continued to do the work, I realized that it was only the beginning. As my own
inner work deepened, I realized that my anxiety and I had some real
qualms about one another that we needed to hash out. Thirty years'
worth of qualms, to be exact. My anxiety wanted to know why, for so
long, I had been ignoring it and all of the ways in which it was trying to
help me. For my part, I wanted to know why it thought it deserved to
take up space in my chest and hinder me and cause extra problems in my
life in so many different ways.

For the first time, I gave my anxiety a voice. I learned that it was
separate from me. We had a conversation. And it actually didn't feel so
bad to listen to it rather than try to outrun it. I apologized for trying to
silence it without listening to it first.

In later chapters, you will address your own qualms about your
anxiety, which will be the impetus to changing your relationship with it.
You will gain a greater understanding of the ways in which anxiety is
actually trying to help you. You will learn to partner with it rather than
feeling at odds with it. You will experience greater freedom in your life
because you will no longer be at war with yourself.

REFLECTION: Resolving Qualms—A Journal Exercise

What do you anticipate needing to share with your anxiety about the way it
has impacted you? Can you start to imagine what grievances your anxiety
might have to share with you? How do you anticipate that having this conversation might impact your relationship with anxiety?

Once I trusted that my anxiety was really trying to help me, and
that there was a real path to healing, I agreed to let my colleague guide
me through what's called a *float back exercise* (a concept from EMDR).
This allowed my anxiety to show me some boulders I had become

tethered to earlier in my life. The roles reversed; I stopped climbing the mountain of life and let anxiety lead me on a descent into the canyon that was my past experiences. This took a tremendous amount of trust and willingness to stop along the way to take breaks. After all, I hadn't taken this route before; it was overwhelming and scary, and it felt contrary to my goal of reaching the top of the mountain. I had to acknowledge my discomfort often; I had to ask anxiety to give me grace in the rate at which I was comfortable descending. Surprisingly, it obliged me, despite my not having reciprocated with that same grace in the preceding years.

Then a memory from when I was five years old hit me like a ton of bricks. *This must have been the biggest boulder that I've been tethered to*, I thought to myself. In this memory, I was sitting at the dinner table with my two older brothers and our mom and dad. My brothers were taking turns quoting lines from a cartoon. I wanted to quote a line that included the phrase "corny details." I got my words mixed up and said "horny details." My brothers, being immature eight- and ten-year-olds, erupted in laughter, and my mom's face turned bright red as she fought back her own giggles. I was dumbfounded. I didn't even know what horny meant. All I knew was I had gotten it wrong. Because everyone was so embarrassed on my behalf, nobody explained to me the error I had made, which would turn out to be the precipitating event for my anxiety decades later when I sat in professional meetings. I had great parents who would have never suggested that I was stupid, but from this experience this is the message that I internalized, along with a firm belief that I shouldn't speak up anymore. I carried this belief within me for nearly thirty years.

Now, in the float back exercise, I kept my eyes closed and allowed myself to really sink into this memory. I was periodically interrupted by my own thoughts, like *Get outta here. This is painful. Why are you doing this?* My colleague had prepared me for the exercise, explaining how to handle my natural responses; accordingly, I noticed these thoughts and returned my attention to the memory. I surrendered to the anxiety and allowed it to show me what it needed to. I remembered all that I could of the memory, which didn't need to be much. It was more about the felt sense of it. And boy, was I feeling it. As I continued the exercise, I felt my throat tightening and moisture welling up in my eyes. *Here we go,* I thought. I leaned into the feeling, and I freely shed tears for that little girl, who felt so rejected at that dinner table. Then, following my colleague's prompts, I imagined my adult self entering this memory with my five-year-old self and giving her what she had needed so badly then but didn't receive: a trusted adult to sit down with her and say "The word *horny* means that you want to have sex. Your brothers are laughing because it's an adult word and they are still kids, which means they are still a little immature. It's actually not even that funny, and you have nothing to worry about. Now let's go do something fun!" I breathed a huge sigh of relief as I pictured my five year old self smiling and hugging me, then the two of us running off to play with dolls. It was everything she needed and never got. And now I was in a position to give it to her, and I did. I'd never experienced anything more powerful in my healing journey than that exercise.

After spending some time with the feelings brought on by this exercise, I opened my eyes and turned my attention back to my colleague, who was looking at me, beaming, with tears in her eyes.

"What the heck did you just do to me?" I asked her.

She laughed. I laughed. And I became a staunch believer in this work.

The experience I had with my younger self that day became foundational to the work I do with my clients. I will teach you the principles and guide you through the same process in later chapters.

Prior to this healing work, I wouldn't have considered that dinner table memory a traumatic one. I had been in therapy before, and this memory was never addressed. I wouldn't have bet that it was traumatic enough to be causing problems in my life all of these years later. But that's the thing about what I call *little t traumas*: they aren't always big, impactful events; rather, they are smaller, less significant ones that produce big feelings that we unknowingly carry with us—feelings that get reinforced over time.

If there's one thing this experience taught me, it was that these kinds of memories matter. It was why, decades later—when I sat in that professional internship meeting and had the thought *What if I sound dumb?*—it felt like my life was ending. It's why, when I tried to rationalize and name things in my environment and challenge my thinking, the anxiety only grew over time. It was the reason my brain was misperceiving threats now. It was a huge boulder in my past that was unresolved and keeping me stuck. That feeling of being dumb, laughed at, and alone was what my anxiety had been trying to protect me from all along.

As you become aware of your own unresolved past experiences, you will gain insight into the ways in which your anxiety is trying to protect you, perhaps from other feelings that are far more painful than anxiety itself. You will acknowledge that you and your anxiety share a common goal, and you don't actually want it to stop doing its job. Rather than trying to terminate it, you can work with your anxiety to modify its job description in a way that makes life easier for you both.

The next couple of chapters will guide you through what I refer to as "the work before the work." You will learn basic anxiety management techniques that will help take the edge off your anxiety temporarily when it's getting in the way of your basic functioning. You will understand the role that avoidance of your anxiety has in preserving it and keeping you stuck. You will also get clear on why the work to come is the best solution for long-term anxiety management.

Next, you will be guided through the work. In chapters 4 through 6 you will engage in exercises that orient you to your anxiety, and you will allow your anxiety to guide you back to the boulders that are keeping you stuck. You will make connections with the younger version of yourself who first experienced these anxiety-provoking experiences. Together you will explore what your younger self needed at that time, and I will guide you through how to provide that now. You will become the source of healing that the younger you has always needed but never gotten until now. You will find that your most powerful resource in healing the source of your anxiety is your current, adult self.

Finally, you will engage in future-oriented work that will help you maintain a working relationship with your anxiety moving forward. You'll establish a communication plan with it so that when it registers a future threat, you can discuss it together and come up with a plan for how to respond. You'll understand what to do if you have an "anxiety relapse," or a time when anxiety does become debilitating again.

I know this is possible because I have experienced these shifts in doing my own work. My anxiety is not gone, but now I don't want it to be. I can see how it works to help me, and it's clear to me that no matter what it's fussing about, we share a common goal of self preservation of some sort. We both want safety, acceptance, belonging, and respect, and when anxiety shows up, it's usually because it feels like one of these things is being threatened. I have become more aware of when it's trying to grab my attention and can engage in dialogue with it that feels productive and helpful to us both. In the context of professional meetings, I am able to soothe my anxiety by imagining soothing that five-year-old little girl. I'm able to safely explore what anxiety needs from me and then work to meet those needs. I can also communicate when I need anxiety to loosen its grip and give me some space, which it now trusts me to do. Since doing this work, we have come up with a mutual agreement for the future: I will listen to and respect it, and it will back off and allow me to engage in professional settings the way I want to be able to—without a crippling fear of rejection. The results have been amazing—and led me to be able to say yes to writing this book.

My hope for you in doing this work is that you will gain the perspective to reframe your anxiety as a helpful force in your life. I understand that at this point it is probably hard to see anything about your anxiety as helpful. Befriending your anxiety might feel like the opposite of what you're used to doing. But stick with me on this journey, and you will find that the willingness to lean into your anxiety rather than avoid it will give you a quality of freedom you've only dreamed of.

A Note for Trauma Survivors

If you have a significant trauma history, are currently experiencing ongoing trauma or threats to your safety, or have diagnosed PTSD or dissociative disorder, it is likely that what will come up in the course of doing this work is outside of the scope of self-help material and will require the support and oversight of a licensed therapist. You may still find the process of befriending your anxiety to be helpful and even transformative, but the guidance of a professional, trauma-informed therapist is essential to keep you safe as you learn and heal. If you're unsure about whether it's safe to proceed, a therapist may be able to do an assessment to help you determine your level of readiness to engage in these types of exercises on your own.

CHAPTER 2

finding your healing window

If you're feeling some combination of hopeful and terrified about learning to befriend your anxiety, you're probably on the right track. Contemplating this work might bring up thoughts like *If I go there, what if I can't make the anxiety stop?* or *What if I remember things from my past that are too much for me to handle?* If you are experiencing such thoughts, you are not alone. And this work *will* inevitably bring up discomfort; if it doesn't, there will be no benefit. The saying "The only way out is through" applies to what we will do together.

That said, the discomfort you experience in the process of working with your anxiety should remain manageable. As I mentioned at the end of the last chapter, if trauma is a significant part of your past or present, you'll need help from a therapist. Diving into past experiences before your nervous system trusts that it's safe to do so can actually cause more harm than benefit. For example, it may be that your brain learned to detach from reality when reality was too overwhelming, and you still experience some dissociation. If so, trying to revisit the experiences that caused dissociation in the first place without proper safety and oversight may cause your brain to want to further detach. Similarly, if you experienced a "freeze" response during a traumatic experience and then you revisit past experiences without an adequate sense of safety, it is highly likely you'll "freeze" again. This is harmful: it reinforces the trauma response rather than fostering its healing.

You will know it is safe to continue this work when you can achieve two things:

- *State change*. This is a term that comes from EMDR therapy. It means you are capable of going from an anxious state to a less anxious state by practicing the tools and techniques outlined in this chapter. You will feel more confident when your anxiety increases if you know you can use a tool like deep breathing to bring it back down again.

- *Dual awareness*. Another term from EMDR therapy, it suggests that when revisiting a trauma memory, you should be able to pay attention to the memory, while not losing sight of the fact that you are in the here and now, where the danger is not currently happening. If you can maintain this perspective, you will likely not experience dissociation or "reliving" the memory. A necessary component of practicing dual awareness is that the here and now is *actually* safe.

This chapter will provide the tools you need to achieve an anxiety state change and maintain dual awareness while doing the work. The skills taught in this chapter are not designed to be problem-solvers. In other words, these skills do not address the root of your anxiety and are not "the work"; rather, they are the work *before* the work. They will not eradicate anxiety or keep you feeling calm over the long term; they are designed to bring you some sense of felt safety in the present moment. Think of these skills as helping you dial down your anxiety.

The work you'll do in this book requires finding the amount of discomfort that is right for you. It is important that you have *some* exposure to anxiety-provoking past experiences, but this should never reach a level that causes you to *relive* past experiences rather than *revisit* them. This concept was described as the "window of tolerance" by Dr. Dan Siegel (1999), and this term is used to describe the optimal zone where healing is possible.

One way to determine if you are within your window of tolerance while doing this work is to assess your concept of time. The goal is to remain cognitively in the present, with an embodied understanding that you are in a time and space that is free of imminent danger, while you are revisiting a memory in which that was not the case. This is dual awareness, and its presence suggests that you are within your optimal window. If at any time you lose orientation to the present time and experience a flashback that causes you to feel like you are actually back in that dangerous time and space without an anchor to the present, you have exited the window of tolerance that is your optimal healing zone. When this happens, it is more likely that you are reinforcing a trauma response rather than healing from it.

Siegel (1999) posits that if you have left your window of tolerance, you are experiencing either *hypoarousal* or *hyperarousal*. Both of these states are a survival response designed to help you survive a threat. Hypoarousal feels like under-stimulation of your nervous system and can include feeling emotionally numb, shut down, detached, or spacey. It is also known as the freeze response. If while doing this work you start to feel detached from your body, excessively tired and shut down, or like you should be experiencing emotions but can't, you might have exited your window of tolerance and could be experiencing hypoarousal.

By contrast, if you experience what feels like overstimulation of your nervous system, like crying combined with hyperventilation, rapid heart rate, shallow breathing, racing thoughts, and/or the impulse to flee, you might be experiencing hyperarousal. This state is referred to as "fight or flight," as your body prepares for action.

Both hypoarousal and hyperarousal are indicators from your nervous system that your sense of safety has been compromised. This can happen as a result of losing dual awareness. In other words, your body starts to think it is actually reexperiencing the trauma rather than remembering it. In an effort to protect you, it kicks you out of your healing zone and into survival mode. Even if you logically know you are safe, treat this as a cue from your body that it needs to feel more safe before proceeding, to avoid harm.

Our window of tolerance is not fixed; it can look different depending on the day and what is going on in our life. Perhaps at one time you are able to do a particular piece of inner work adequately and safely, staying in your healing zone. However, outside factors such as additional life stressors, sleep deprivation, certain medications, and/or hormone imbalances may create increased sensitivities and make you more vulnerable to being emotionally overwhelmed. Perhaps the most important part of this work is an ongoing assessment and honoring of your capacity to do it.

You will know you are within your window of tolerance when you have access to both your emotions and your logic. Being inside the healing window does not mean you will experience an absence of emotion. Remember that the goal is to experience the right amount of emotion for you in your healing work—it feels uncomfortable, yet tolerable and balanced by logic. Refer to this chart to help you determine whether you are in your window of tolerance or experiencing hyper- or hypoarousal.

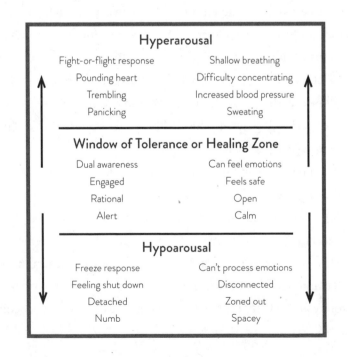

Hyperarousal

Fight-or-flight response	Shallow breathing
Pounding heart	Difficulty concentrating
Trembling	Increased blood pressure
Panicking	Sweating

Window of Tolerance or Healing Zone

Dual awareness	Can feel emotions
Engaged	Feels safe
Rational	Open
Alert	Calm

Hypoarousal

Freeze response	Can't process emotions
Feeling shut down	Disconnected
Detached	Zoned out
Numb	Spacey

This chapter is designed to teach you some anxiety-regulation strategies to help keep you in the healing zone by establishing and maintaining a felt sense of safety in your body. You can use these skills while engaging in this work; they can also be useful in your day-to-day life when you're working to regulate an anxiety response. These skills are not designed to be one-size-fits-all; what may be effective for one person might not work for another. In figuring out what works for you, it can be helpful to try a variety of different regulation strategies and keep a log or journal of your experiences, rating each for how effective they were for you, on a scale of 0 to 10.

The varying degree of effectiveness of these skills is highly dependent on your unique experiences, anxiety triggers, and preferences. When trying these skills or other anxiety-regulation practices, aim for breadth rather than depth. The more exercises you try, the more likely it is that you'll find the skills that are useful for you and can be added to your anxiety-management repertoire. It's helpful to try these skills while your anxiety is low and manageable, even if you think to yourself, *I don't have much anxiety right now; why would I need to practice these skills?* When our anxiety is high, it's likely that our fight-flight-freeze response is activated; when that's the case, it becomes incredibly difficult to problem solve and try a new skill. If, when your anxiety is high, you have already practiced these and discovered what works for you, you will require less innovation and troubleshooting in the moment and will feel more automatic, making it more likely these tools will be effective for you.

Self-Soothing

Self-soothing skills are exactly what they sound like: exercises designed to soothe your nervous system. Our five best-known senses (smell, hearing, taste, touch, and sight) play a large role in how our brains assess and respond to threats. For example, if you experience the felt sense of something crawling on your leg, and you are afraid of bugs, you are likely to immediately register some amount of danger and swat at your leg to remove the threat. If you have a bee phobia (or allergy) and hear a buzzing sound hovering around your ear, you will likely associate that sound with some amount of danger and run away (maybe for the hills). If you see or smell smoke coming from inside your home, your nervous system will do its job in recognizing that sight or smell as dangerous and will prompt you for action. You can see how our senses play an integral role in our sense of safety; they are designed to be the first line of defense against a threat by sounding the alarm. If our survival brains become activated by input through our five senses, it makes good sense that by soothing our senses we can in turn soothe our nervous systems.

What's soothing to me might be very different from what feels soothing to you based on your own unique experiences and past associations, which is why it's important to approach this with an open mind and confidence that you can recognize what's best for you.

Here are some examples of activities or objects that can feel soothing, broken down by the five senses.

Activities That Might Soothe Your Sense of Smell

- Baking bread
- Lighting a scented candle
- Going for a walk after it's rained
- Smelling fresh-cut flowers at a florist or grocery store
- Smelling freshly washed and dried linens
- Diffusing lavender or peppermint essential oils
- Smelling crisp mountain air
- Smelling coffee beans
- Smelling freshly popped popcorn

- Smelling sweet basil

- Smelling lemon balm

- Hanging an air freshener in your car

- Cooking with lemon zest, herbs, and spices

Sounds That Might Soothe Your Sense of Hearing

- Water sounds (ocean, rainfall, thunderstorms)

- Instrumental, ambient, or jazz music

- Humming sounds (engines, motors, fans, white noise)

- Laughter

- Hoofbeats

- Flutes, drums, or violin

- Chanting

- Crunching

- Shaking of a spray can

- A paintbrush stroking a canvas

- Gentle whispering

- Crash of pins from a strike in bowling

- Pages of a book being turned

Activities That Might Soothe Your Sense of Taste

- Eating a favorite childhood meal or snack

- Chewing peppermint gum

- Eating a popsicle on a hot day

- Eating dark chocolate

- Drinking hot tea with honey

- Drinking hot water with lemon

- Eating fresh fruits like oranges, mangoes, or strawberries

- Drinking hot coffee or warm milk with cinnamon

- Eating juicy fruits like watermelon, pineapple, and peaches

- Eating warm bread with butter

- Drinking cold lemonade

- Sipping hot soup

Activities That Might Soothe Your Sense of Touch

- Walking barefoot in the sand

- Getting a shoulder or foot massage

- Covering yourself with a fuzzy or weighted blanket

- Feeling the cool breeze on your face

- Petting your dog or cat

- Getting a tight squeeze hug from a loved one

- Stroking or massaging your hair and scalp

- Playing with Play-Doh or sand

- Wearing a soft sweater and noticing how it feels against your skin

- Popping bubble wrap

- Lying in blankets fresh from the hot dryer

- Walking on dried leaves or pinecones

- Holding grounding stones in your hand

- Lying on an acupressure mat

- Getting into a hot tub or bath with jets

Activities That Might Soothe Your Sense of Sight

- Looking at photos of baby animals

- Looking at photos of loved ones or people you admire

- Looking at nature (mountains, ocean, forest)

- Watching clouds go by

- Stargazing

- Bird watching

- Watching a lava lamp

- Looking at the colors of autumn leaves

- Watching the sunrise or sunset

- Watching video of a turning windmill

- Looking at art in a museum

- Watching someone paint

- Watching someone draw straight lines

- Watching someone concentrate

- Looking through color swatches

- Looking at Christmas lights

- Watching wood burning in a fireplace

If you can create these experiences in your current environment, that is great. If not, it can be just as effective to soothe your sense of sight or hearing by watching or listening to videos of these experiences on the internet. You will need to engage in these activities and practices mindfully to get the most out of them. For example, if you take a walk after it's rained but spend the entire walk talking on the phone, you may completely miss the soothing post-rain smell (there's a name for that smell: petrichor!) and will likely not benefit from the exercise as much as you might have if you were mindfully noticing your surroundings.

When you have had a chance to experiment with some of these sensory self-soothing techniques, reflect in your journal on what worked for you and what else you might try. This exercise offers some prompts.

REFLECTION: Self-Soothing—A Journal Exercise

1. Which of my five senses was easiest for me to soothe? Most challenging?

2. Which self-soothing techniques worked well for me?

3. Which self-soothing practices didn't work so well?

4. How did I know when something was soothing for me?

5. What might I try next time I want to self-soothe using my five senses?

Finding Your Calm Place

A potentially powerful anxiety-regulation strategy involves visualizing a place that you either have been or imagine being that feels exceptionally calming. The idea of an internal calm place is drawn from Francine Shapiro (2001), who called it your "safe place." Your calm place can be something as simple and familiar as your bed or as extravagant as a Greek isle. It can be a real place that you frequent or an imaginary, fairytale-like scene from your favorite Disney movie. The specific location matters less than the felt sense you get when you are there or imagine being there. The most important part of this exercise is that the place feels calming and soothing to your nervous system. Once you have a place in mind, you can begin the exercise. It's helpful to read through the whole exercise before you begin; you can also find an audio version to download in the online free tools at http://www.newharbinger.com/48756.

EXERCISE: Calm Place Visualization

Find a place in your home or office that is free of distractions. Sit or lie comfortably and start by turning your attention toward your breath. Take note of the sensations you notice as the air travels in through your nostrils and into your lungs, then is released through your nose or mouth. Take a couple of breaths here.

Now bring up the image of your calm place. Imagine yourself in this place, where you feel completely calm and completely safe. Begin to experience this place through your five senses, starting with sight. Experience this place through your eyes. What do you see? Take note of the colors this calm place has to offer. Now notice the shapes. Pay attention to any other sights this soothing place offers. Take a moment here. Breathe. If you notice stray thoughts entering, that's okay. Just acknowledge them and turn your attention back to your calm place.

Now turn your attention to your sense of hearing. Notice the sounds present in this calm place. Perhaps you hear wind or water. Maybe there are trees rustling. Maybe you notice a quiet hum, or perhaps it's completely silent. Take note of all of the different sounds you experience in this calm place, both near and far. Pause for a moment here.

Next, notice your sense of smell. What smells does this calm place have to offer? Perhaps you can smell crisp, clean air. Maybe you smell freshly baked bread coming from the oven. Maybe you're taking in the smell of wildflowers or salty ocean water. Allow yourself to fully experience this place through your nose. Notice.

Now turn your attention to your sense of taste. First, notice the moisture in your mouth. If you'd like, imagine sipping your favorite beverage or eating a delicious snack in this calm, soothing place. Savor the flavors as you imagine nourishing your body with this food or drink. If you find yourself distracted, simply notice the distraction and gently turn your attention back to your senses.

Finally, pay attention to your sense of touch. Notice the temperature on your skin. Do you feel the warmth of the sun, or perhaps a cool breeze? Can you notice how your clothes feel as they rest against your skin? Notice the surface that supports you. Maybe you are sitting in the grass, cool and damp, or beach sand that shifts and molds to your body. Perhaps you're lying on a cloud, or in your warm, comfortable bed. What textures are nearby that you can reach out and touch? Imagine touching them. Experience this calm place fully through the sensation of touch. Breathe.

Experience this calm place through all five of these senses. Remain in this place for as long as you'd like, taking in all it has to offer. If you'd like to revisit one of the senses in particular, return your focus there now. When you're ready to reorient yourself in the present moment, take a mental snapshot of yourself in this calm place. This image will serve as a reminder of this place, which you can return to at any time when you need a mental break. Now gradually begin to open your eyes and return your attention to your surroundings.

Once you've tried the calm place visualization one or more times, reflect in your journal on your experience. This will help you solidify your sense of how helpful this visualization is as a tool for you to self-soothe.

REFLECTION: Calm Place—A Journal Exercise

1. Where is your calm place? What was that experience like for you?

2. Which of the five senses felt most easily accessible to you? Which one brought the greatest sense of calm?

3. Did you notice any internal or external distractions? Were you able to acknowledge them and return your attention to the exercise?

4. How effective was this exercise in soothing your nervous system?

5. Would you return to this particular calm place, or would you choose another? What about this calm place did you like, and what didn't work for you?

My favorite thing about the calm place visualization is its versatility. It can be scheduled into your day as a twenty-minute mindfulness practice, or it can be done as a thirty-second exercise on the fly when you need a time-out from a stressful day. It can be done from a yoga mat rolled out on your living room floor, or in your car, or at the office. The important thing about the exercise is that it remains a calm place that feels soothing to your senses.

If for any reason your calm place becomes compromised and no longer feels calming, you'll want to pick a different place rather than force this place to feel soothing again. For example, you might begin to imagine last year's vacation destination, which starts off as very calming, but then your mind starts to wander and you begin to feel shame because of how you acted last time you were on vacation there. Now this calm place has a negative association, and you may need to pick an alternate place.

Returning to the Present

To be oriented to the present time is to experience the world through the eyes of your most current, present self rather than from a younger version. Many times, especially when we are experiencing anxiety or another emotion that doesn't fit the facts of the situation we're in, we are not totally oriented to the present. Anxiety often manifests as worry about the future, which might lead us to believe that when we are anxious, we are living in the future rather than in the present. While it is true that anxiety can cause future-oriented thinking, it is usually a symptom of some unresolved, distressing past experience. For example, if when I was twenty I was told by someone I trusted and thought was my friend that they didn't actually like me at all, this memory may be an unresolved little t trauma that affects my emotions in social situations now. Let's say that I'm now twenty-six, beginning to establish a close relationship with a new friend, and having difficulty trusting this friend because of my past experience. I am likely engaging in this current friendship from the eyes of my twenty-year-old self rather than my twenty-six-year-old self, which may cause me to be wary and guarded. In this scenario, I might be rationally aware that I'm twenty-six now and this is a completely different friend who has never caused me to distrust her, but my emotional experience of fear and anxiety may suggest that I am not completely oriented to the present time.

The work in chapters 4 through 6 involves taking a deeper dive and revisiting those past experiences to untether yourself from them. For the purposes of the work before the work, it's important to understand the difference between being time oriented and disoriented, and to get some practice orienting yourself to the present time.

To be oriented to the present time does not mean you will not experience emotions; rather, it means you will experience emotions that fit the facts of your current situation. For example, if you experience anxiety before giving an important presentation at work, this does not automatically mean that you are disoriented to the present time, even if you've had a past distressing experience with presentations. To be human is to experience emotions, and emotions are often helpful, necessary cues that can tell us important things about our values. In this case, it is possible that you would experience some anxiety before giving a presentation because the presentation is important to you and you want to do well. Perhaps the anxiety would be helpful in the week prior to the presentation because it would prompt you to do your research and prepare thoroughly. It might even be helpful to you on the day of the presentation if it prompted you to leave the house with enough time to find parking and review your notes beforehand. You can see how it's possible to experience anxiety and still be oriented to the present time.

When revisiting past distressing experiences, the goal is to have one foot in the present and one foot in the past. This concept—the dual awareness described earlier—was introduced by Francine Shapiro in 1995. With dual awareness, while we might experience the emotions associated with past distressing events while revisiting them, we never lose sight of the fact that we are reflecting on memories, and the danger is not currently happening. When we become overwhelmed or flooded with emotion that doesn't fit the facts of our current situation, it is likely that we have both feet in either the past or the future, rather than one foot here and one foot there. When we don't have *either* foot in the present, our nervous system will register a need for safety and activate a survival response, pushing us out of our healing zone. We can reestablish safety by using time orientation skills to pull ourselves back into the present moment, where there is no danger.

There's one essential component of practicing time orientation: it needs to be done when there is actually no present threat. If there is one, orienting yourself to the present will not be soothing and could cause more harm. For example, let's say you have a fear of dogs that stems from being bitten by a dog when you were ten years old. Now you're twenty-four, walking in a park. In the distance you see someone walking a dog on a leash—one that looks very much like the dog that bit you. You are hit with a strong wave of anxiety. In this situation, time orientation skills would help your nervous system get on board with what your logic already knows: that this leashed dog, walking fifty feet away, is very unlikely to harm you. These skills would allow you to focus on things in your present environment that are different from the experience you had when you were ten, and they provide evidence that you're not facing the same threat now, thereby soothing your nervous system.

Now let's say you are walking in a dark alley and all of a sudden you see a dog running toward you. The dog is alone, no owner in sight; it must be a stray. And it's acting aggressive: lips drawn back from its fangs, growling and snarling. In this case, it does not make any sense to practice time orientation skills, because the present situation is dangerous.

The more you tried to orient yourself to time—*what's actually happening, here and now*—the more danger you would feel. What's more helpful (and what is likely to happen automatically) is that your survival instincts kick in and you respond accordingly by either running away or defending yourself. If you feel anxiety the following day when walking through that same dark alley—however, this time there is no dog in sight—time orientation skills would prove useful again.

If you are experiencing anxiety that does not fit the facts or feels disproportionate to your current situation and there is no current danger or threat, time orientation skills will be useful. Time orientation skills are even more accessible than the calm place visualization, because you can practice them anywhere, and the people around you won't necessarily even know when you are practicing them. These skills involve turning your attention toward anything in your present environment, where there is no danger.

The benefits of time orientation are twofold. First, adopting a regular practice of orienting to the present time helps train you to approach life more mindfully. Decades of research have shown that regular mindfulness practice can improve both emotional and physical health via reducing anxiety and depression and improving emotion regulation. Time orientation exercises are also helpful because we humans are not good multitaskers; when we are given a mental task like listing things in our environment, we don't do very well at simultaneously ruminating about the past or worrying about the future. A common example of this phenomenon is when you're talking on the phone with someone, listening intently, and then someone nearby asks you a question and you suddenly realize you missed part of what the person on the phone said. We don't do well with paying attention to two things at once, despite what we'd like to believe, but this deficit serves us well when we want to shift our attention away from something triggering.

Here are two specific time orientation techniques that I encourage you to try:

- *Name ten things that you can see right here, right now.* These can be as general as a tree you can see nearby or as detailed and specific as the different shades of green on a patch of lawn nearby. Here's an example: in this current moment, while practicing time orientation, I noticed the numbers on the barcode on my bottle of water. The last four digits are the same numbers as the last four digits of my childhood home's phone number. This is something I never would have noticed had I not been intentionally practicing time orientation. The more detailed you can be in your observations, the better.

- *Mentally list details that serve as evidence that you are not your younger self.* Someone I once knew had childhood trauma that happened on the East Coast, where there is a very different climate than in Arizona, where she later resided. Whenever she experienced a trigger and needed to orient to the present time, she would go outside and look at the cacti and other features of the desert landscape around her. It helped her nervous system remember by providing evidence that she was in a completely different time and space—all the way across the country—from where the danger happened.

If you were a child or adolescent when the danger happened, notice the things in your life that point to your now being an adult. Perhaps you have bills lying on your kitchen table that you need to pay, or a grocery list posted on your refrigerator. These items can serve as anchors to the present time, providing evidence that you are older and no longer threatened in the same way. If the trauma happened before you could drive and you now have a car, turn your attention to your car: pull out your registration and driver's license and let these serve as a reminder that you have more resources now than you did then. If, since the trauma, you have a new supportive person in your life who provides safety and comfort, give them a call and allow them to support you, while noticing that this is a resource that didn't exist for you in the past. Anything that can serve as evidence of your different life circumstances in the current time that wasn't present at the time of the trauma can be a useful tool for time orientation.

REFLECTION: Time Orientation—A Journal Exercise

Give time orientation skills a try. What are ten details about your current environment you can notice now? They could be objects, colors, activities, sounds, smells, temperature. Write them in your journal.

Next, reflect in your journal on the following questions. These will help empower you to practice time orientation skills the next time a mismatch between your past or future and your present situation is causing you unnecessary distress.

- When would be a good time for me to practice time orientation skills?

- How will I know if my attention is in the past and I need to orient myself to the present?

- How will I know if I am worrying about a future scenario and need to pull myself back to the present?

- What are some people, places, or things that I can use to orient myself to the present?

- What is different about my life now from when things were more distressing?

Diaphragm Breathing

When it comes to regulating anxiety, there is no more powerful tool than your own breath. There are two main types of breathing: chest breathing and diaphragm breathing. Chest breathing is more shallow and occurs naturally when your body needs to get in a lot of oxygen quickly, such as after a sprint. When you are chest breathing, you'll be able to see and feel your chest rise and fall with each breath. Diaphragm breathing, also called belly breathing, involves breathing more deeply into your lungs; this causes your diaphragm—which is located below your lungs near the bottom of your ribcage—to flex downward, pushing out your abdomen. When you are breathing diaphragmatically, you should see your belly rising and falling with each breath, with little movement in your chest.

Our breathing and our survival response have a reciprocal relation-ship, each having influence over the other. For example, if you encoun-ter a mountain lion on a hike, your fight-or-flight response is likely going to become activated, and your breathing will become more shallow and rapid to increase oxygen flow quickly and prepare you for action. This is an example of hyperarousal. Chest breathing is helpful in this situation, when there is a real threat of bodily harm, as it increases your chances of fending off danger and making it out alive. When we live with anxiety, we may register threats that don't actually exist or that exist on a much smaller scale than we are perceiving. This causes us to breathe in a way that prepares and encourages us to fight or flee when actually there is no danger. This can become a vicious cycle that perpetuates and reinforces anxiety over time. Perceived threat → anxiety → chest breathing → more anxiety caused by chest breathing → new perceived threats, and so on. Similarly to how you can communicate safety to your survival brain through self-soothing with your senses, by breathing deeply into the dia-phragm you can help convey to yourself that the danger you perceived doesn't really exist. Breathing deeply activates the parasympathetic nervous system, which is in charge of regulating emotions and calming you down.

There are two ways I like to practice diaphragm breathing. The first is the hand method, a simple trick that helps gauge whether you're breathing into your chest or diaphragm. To practice this method, sit comfortably upright with your feet flat on the floor. Start by placing one hand on your upper chest and the other hand on your abdomen, just below your navel. As you breathe in through your nose, notice the movement of your hands. Try to breathe in deeply enough that the hand on your belly moves outward as your belly expands with each inhale, while the hand on your chest moves very little. Continue breathing deeply, trying to move the hand on your belly more than the one on your chest. When you achieve this, you'll know you are breathing into your diaphragm.

The second way to practice diaphragm breathing is called *box breathing* or *four-square breathing*. By either name, this technique has been used since the 1980s by the Navy SEALs and in other high-stress professions such as nursing and policing (Stinson, 2018). It is used to exit fight-or-flight mode and for general soothing, recentering, and concentration of the mind. To practice box breathing, find a comfortable position seated in a chair with your feet flat on the floor. Close your eyes and breathe in through your nose to the count of four, noticing the sensations of the breath entering your nostrils and lungs. Hold your breath in your lungs to the count of four, and then begin to slowly exhale to the count of four. After exhaling, pause for four seconds before starting your next inhale. Repeat this for several minutes. It can be helpful to picture a box while engaging in this exercise, like the one shown here.

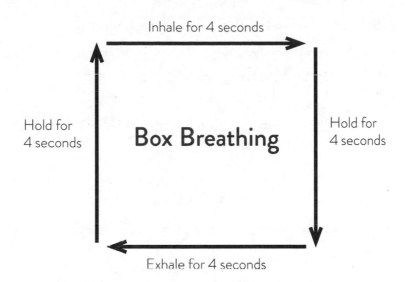

REFLECTION: Diaphragm Breathing—A Journal Exercise

1. What were these breathing exercises like for me?

2. How can I tell when I am chest breathing versus diaphragm breathing?

3. Which breathing exercise was more effective for me: the hand method or box breathing?

4. When is a good time for me to practice diaphragm breathing?

5. How does breathing play a role in my experience with anxiety?

REFLECTION: Taking It All In—A Journal Exercise

Take some time to reflect on what you've learned in this chapter and how it's affected your experience with your anxiety, and record your answers in your journal.

1. Which of the anxiety-regulation strategies in this chapter were most helpful? Least helpful?

2. Are there other anxiety regulation strategies, not listed here, that have been helpful to me in the past? If so, what are they?

3. How will I know when I am in need of increased safety in my body and mind?

4. When do I experience anxiety most frequently? Which of these skills might be useful in those instances?

5. As I move forward with the work, how will I know when I need to take a break and return to these skills?

6. What more do I need to practice before moving on to the work?

My hope is that these practices will help you to feel more empowered in your ability to regulate your anxiety, in addition to equipping you to do the work of making peace with your anxiety by increasing the felt sense of safety in your body and mind. These tools have been proven effective at reducing anxiety in the moment; however, without getting to the source of why your brain is registering a threat that doesn't actually exist, the anxiety will always return. I suggest you think of these tools as helping with symptom reduction rather than addressing the root of the problem. When we use these tools as a long-term solution and replacement for doing the work, what may feel like a start at skillfully coping can morph into avoiding.

You should expect to revisit this chapter throughout the course of this work. Healing anxiety is messy and usually does not follow a linear path. As you are working through subsequent chapters, you may find that you have exited your healing window and are reliving past experiences. Or you may just want a break from the heaviness of the work. When this happens, return to this chapter and these practices. You may even find that you want to continue practicing these skills for months before moving on to later chapters. That is okay! Or you may feel ready to move forward with the work now. Move forward at your own pace, remembering always to tune in, assess your felt sense of safety, and honor it, even if you wish it were different.

Now that you have learned skills to help you temporarily take the edge off your anxiety, you are prepared to move on to the next step in the work: exploring avoidance, the primary behavior that keeps anxiety stuck. In the following chapter, you'll learn to distinguish the difference between helpful and problematic avoidance. Once you learn the difference, I'll help you let go of the latter, which will move you one step closer to healing your relationship with anxiety for good.

CHAPTER 3

avoiding avoidance

All humans are hard-wired to avoid pain. It is natural for us to avoid painful conversations, experiences, and emotions, even if we know we will probably be better off long-term if we confront them. Avoidance is a defensive, protective strategy we're conditioned to use from a very young age, as it is a necessary part of survival. For example, when a toddler learns that touching a hot stove is very painful, he will likely avoid touching the stove again in the future. This is a necessary adaptation. Similarly, if a child learns that expressing her emotions is unsafe because when she cries her parents become increasingly agitated and tell her "Big girls don't cry," she will likely try to avoid crying in the future, in an effort to appease her caregivers and skillfully adapt to her environment. If she doesn't adapt in this way, she may be subjected to more disapproval and ridicule, which all children want to avoid. While stuffing emotions in this way is a behavior that can cause major problems later in life, in an environment in which emotional expression leads to compromised safety, avoidance of emotions may prove useful.

Another example of learned avoidance shows up when school-aged children discover what will help them fit in with a group. For example, if they find that if they wear a certain type of clothing or bring a certain type of lunch to school they will be teased by their classmates, any child will likely want to avoid wearing this type of clothing or bringing this kind of food in the future, to prevent the intensely painful emotions that teasing instigates. If the child is able to convince their parent to pack them a different kind of lunch or buy them a pair of the kind of shoes the other kids wear, it may be effective in reducing bullying. Of course, it is never a child's responsibility to make changes that reduce the likelihood that other humans will be mean to them; the responsibility to change falls on the person or people inflicting harm. However, this example gives insight into the ways in which avoidance of painful emotions is a deeply engrained, often automatic and effective attempt to protect our well-being.

By the time we're adults, we're usually pros at avoidance. We have had many years of experience avoiding what's painful or uncomfortable, and often avoidance behaviors are successful in helping us align with our goals. For example, you may have learned to avoid dating people who exhibit certain red flags early in a relationship, which helps you avoid later conflict or pain. Maybe you are lactose intolerant and have learned to avoid dairy ice cream, despite how much you love it, to prevent inevitable physical discomfort later. Perhaps you've learned to avoid shopping on Amazon when you've had one too many glasses of wine, which prevents you from feeling buyer's remorse the next day. All of these avoidance behaviors are useful because they prevent harm, sometimes by delaying short-term gratification in exchange for caring for ourself long-term.

Helpful Avoidance Versus Problematic Avoidance

Just as there are two types of anxiety, there are two types of avoidance: helpful, necessary avoidance, and avoidance that feels helpful in the short term but causes long-term problems. Throughout this book, I'll refer to these two types as *helpful avoidance* or *problematic avoidance*. Helpful avoidance can be obvious—like avoiding touching a hot stove— and easily accomplished with little inner conflict, or it can require delaying some short-term gratification for a long-term goal, like avoiding a potential relationship partner who excites us but exhibits clear red flags of emotional volatility. In the latter example, we can identify this as helpful avoidance because while it requires enduring the short-term discomfort of saying no to a date with this exciting person, it may help us align with our long-term values of finding a stable, dependable partner.

Problematic avoidance is avoidance that has the opposite effect of helpful avoidance: it prevents discomfort in the short term, but over time moves us further away from our goals rather than helping us become more aligned with them. For example, let's say you experience social anxiety, and one week ago you agreed to attend a friend's birthday party. The day of the party arrives, and as you are getting ready to go you begin to experience heightened anxiety. You may have an inner dialogue that goes something like *I could probably make up an excuse for why I'm not able to make it*, followed by *No, I should go. This friend came to my birthday party and it's important to me to maintain this friendship*, followed by *But imagine how much better I'll feel if I just cancel.*

Sound familiar? And as this inner dialogue continues, it is likely that your anxiety continues to heighten. By the time you need to leave for the party, your anxiety might be so uncomfortable that you will do anything to reduce it, so you impulsively send your friend a text message to say you aren't feeling well and can't make it to the party.

It is very likely that this avoidance behavior is going to instantly reduce your discomfort. You might have a thought like *Thank goodness I don't have to feel that anxiety anymore. I'm so relieved.*

At this stage, it can be hard to identify this type of avoidance as problematic because it feels *so* right. After all, it may have been the only coping strategy out of several you've tried that was effective in reducing your anxiety. However, the next morning when you wake up, begin to scroll social media, and see photos posted from the party, with several people you would have loved to see all having fun together, you are likely to experience some unpleasant emotions. This is when you might start to identify your avoidance as problematic, because while it was effective in helping you avoid anxiety in the short term, it leaves you feeling worse the next day.

This type of avoidance can be problematic for two reasons. First, it involves short-term gratification, which produces an immediate but fleeting benefit that quickly wears off and is replaced with a painful emotion. The painful emotion is usually an indicator that you have not acted in accordance with your values. For example, if attending the party was in line with your values of being socially connected and a supportive friend, your avoidance of it might create feelings of missing out (FOMO), guilt, or shame.

The second reason this type of avoidance is problematic is the behavioral reinforcement it causes. Assuming there is no real threat associated with attending the party, when you are getting ready for it and experiencing heightening anxiety, your survival brain is registering a threat that doesn't actually exist. It's the anxious part of you that says things like *It's going to be awful. Just cancel. You'll feel so much better if you do.* This voice becomes louder and louder the more you try to counter it, because it thinks there is serious danger ahead if you do attend, and it is working hard to protect you from that danger. (In the following chapters, we'll explore together *why* your anxiety registers a threat that isn't really there, and how to help it recalibrate.)

As the tension between your logical brain and anxious voice increases, so do your heart palpitations, sweaty palms, chest breathing, rapid-fire thoughts, and other manifestations of anxiety you might experience. As soon as you send the text message saying you won't make it, the pressure is off, and your anxiety heaves a great sigh of relief: *Oh, thank goodness you listened to me. I'm trying to protect you! Don't you see how dangerous that would have been? I hope you realize you feel safe now because you listened to me. Best to let me take the lead in the future.* This narrative strengthens and reinforces the need to avoid in the future. Not only are you left feeling guilt about missing out on the party, but it will become just a tad bit harder to avoid avoidance the next time you're invited to a social gathering, because your brain has now made the connection that canceling plans = short-term relief from anxiety.

If you have social anxiety, you know that social encounters are usually not as bad as we build them up to be in our heads. When we do attend social events despite having anxiety, it usually reinforces the connection that following through with plans = not that bad, and we may even end up feeling glad we went.

Over time, problematic avoidance convinces us that the only way to reduce anxiety is to avoid hard things, even if it means abandoning our values. But learning how to avoid avoidance helps us build a life consistent with our values.

REFLECTION: On Avoidance—A Journal Exercise

Take some time to reflect on your experience of avoidance—both helpful and problematic—and any patterns that emerge. Record your answers to these questions in your journal.

I.   What things did you learn to avoid as a child that were helpful?

2.   What things did you learn to avoid as a child that were problematic?

3.   As an adult, in what ways do you practice helpful avoidance?

4.   As an adult, in what ways do you practice problematic avoidance?

5.   In what ways does problematic avoidance threaten your values?

Self-Care Versus Avoidance

If you have been in therapy or done any reading about emotional health in the last several years, you have likely been exposed to the concept of self-care and the role it has in preserving mental health. Self-care is the practice of making decisions that prioritize our physical and emotional health. Self-care has become a hot topic in the last few years, both inside and outside of the therapy office. From the very first therapy session, therapists usually assess for the extent to which their clients are practicing care for themselves. After listening to the challenges their client is having that have brought them to therapy, a therapist will likely ask some version of "What are you doing in your day-to-day life to help you cope with these stressors?" Self-care practices are not limited to but can include the following:

- Taking care of basic needs (getting adequate sleep, eating well, taking medications as prescribed, drinking enough water, and so on)

- Practicing mindfulness or meditation

- Exercising or moving your body

- Spending time with friends or loved ones

- Journaling

- Engaging in enjoyable hobbies or activities

- Going on vacation

- Carving out "you" time for whatever makes you feel good

- Treating yourself to something that you don't normally indulge in, like an overpriced coffee

Self-care isn't limited to just bubble baths and fancy coffee drinks. It often includes practices that don't necessarily feel good while you're doing them, but are conducive to caring for yourself long-term, like:

- Scheduling and attending doctor and dentist appointments

- Setting boundaries with others

- Saying no to activities that deplete you

- Tackling responsibilities rather than procrastinating

- Prioritizing sleep over a night out

Self-care is very important, because adequate self-care practices can be an important starting strategy for managing anxiety. For example, let's say you are in therapy to address work-related anxiety. During the course of therapy your therapist learns that you often arrive early and stay late into the evenings at work in order to meet project deadlines, and to make this possible, you are skipping breakfast and missing your evening yoga class. Your therapist is likely going to see a need for improved self-care and might work with you on setting boundaries around your work hours; for example, having you make a commitment to eating breakfast every day and attending your yoga class at least a few times per week. It is likely that with improved self-care practices, your work-related anxiety will start to feel more manageable.

Similarly, if you are in therapy to address poor self-image, and in the course of therapy your therapist learns that you feel particularly bad about yourself after you spend time with a certain friend who often makes negative comments about your weight or appearance and who does not respect the boundaries you set, your therapist may well encourage you to reevaluate how much time you spend with this friend or whether you want to continue this friendship at all. It could be that your self-image begins to improve once you no longer spend as much time with this so-called friend. Bolstering self-care can serve as the first problem-solving approach in your larger effort to reduce anxiety.

While self-care is undoubtedly a necessary ingredient in the recipe for emotional health, the term has begun to be used to describe behaviors that appear on the surface to be self-care, but upon further exploration are actually avoidance in disguise. This can be problematic because we might think we're doing something helpful for ourselves when in reality we are reinforcing and perpetuating the anxiety cycle.

For example, let's say that you feel very overwhelmed with all of your responsibilities. You decide that it would be helpful to engage in a self-care practice, so you turn on your favorite show on Netflix. This may be a helpful, necessary exercise in carving out time to do something enjoyable for yourself and reduce the feeling of being overwhelmed. However, let's say one episode turns into a six-hour binge watch because each time you remember your to-do list it feels too overwhelming, so rather than thinking about it, you continue to watch more episodes. This practice may have started as necessary self-care but turned into avoidance once it started to serve the function of helping you avoid being overwhelmed rather than adding enjoyment to your life.

Let's say you are trying to distract yourself from the feeling of anxiety, and in an effort to do so, you go impulsively spend $300 at Target. This is likely an avoidance behavior rather than a self-care behavior because it's helping you run away from anxiety. However, if you recently completed an important work project and want to celebrate your accomplishment by treating yourself to an uninterrupted Target shopping trip, even if you spend $300 this behavior likely does not serve the same purpose of helping you avoid discomfort; it may be true self-care.

If you are prone to social anxiety, you may be tempted to label your isolation from others as taking care of yourself when in reality it may be that, given your unique circumstances, taking care of yourself actually requires you to do what's harder: persuading yourself to spend time with a friend. On the flip side, if you are introverted and require regular quiet alone time, perhaps choosing to skip out on plans with a friend and enjoy some solitude at home *is* actually an act of self-care. If you engage in compulsive exercise and call it taking care of your body, but the behavior is serving the function of helping you temper body-related obsessions, it is likely that engaging in compulsive exercise is a form of avoidance rather than true self-care. However, setting boundaries at work so you can leave on time to get to your workout class as a means to care for your body may be true self-care.

It can be challenging to distinguish between self-care and avoidance behaviors because the exact same behavior can be a self-care practice for one person and an avoidance strategy for another person. Additionally, the exact same behavior can be an act of self-care for you at one time but an act of avoidance at another time. It is important to ask yourself what function the behavior serves in order to determine if it is a true self-care practice or avoidance in disguise. To get a better idea, you may ask yourself the questions in the following exercise.

REFLECTION: Are Your Self-Care Practices Helping or Harming? A Journal Exercise

Take some time to reflect on your self-care habits, and record your answers to these questions in your journal.

- What are my go-to self-care practices? In other words, what practices do I most rely on to care for my physical and emotional health?

- Does my self-care practice feel like it's soothing my emotions— or helping me detach from them?

- After I engage in this self-care practice, do I feel energized and refreshed or more anxious?

- Do I engage in self-care impulsively to avoid discomfort, or do I plan my self-care activity ahead of time?

- Does my self-care practice feel like coping or escaping?

If a behavior that helps you detach or distract from painful emotions later causes you to feel more discomfort, or you do it impulsively, or it feels like an escape, it could be that it is actually avoidance rather than true self-care. By contrast, if the behavior is planned ahead of time, soothes your emotions, helps you cope with them, and/or leaves you feeling good afterward, that is a good indicator that it is true self-care. Behaviors that are likely to be avoidance in disguise include avoiding responsibilities for days, isolating from supportive people, practicing impulsive "feel-good" behaviors that leave you feeling worse off later, and subjecting yourself to continuous hurt in a relationship for fear of conflict.

We all engage in problematic avoidance from time to time, and it does not always have big consequences in our lives. For example, maybe I push off all my responsibilities on Saturday and binge Netflix instead, which means I have to cram all my weekend to-dos into Sunday afternoon. This is somewhat problematic, because I'm not going to feel great about it on Sunday, but at the same time, it likely won't cause dire problems in my life if I *can* tend to everything on Sunday. For this reason, I might not feel very motivated to dig deep into my behavior to explore the function of this pattern and try to change it. However, when avoidance takes over as the strategy we keep relying on for coping with anxiety and starts to reinforce and perpetuate the anxiety cycle, we need to acknowledge that we're avoiding and see what we can do instead that might be more effective.

REFLECTION: On Self-Care—A Journal Exercise

Reflect on this deeper dive into different kinds of self-care, and record your answers in your journal.

1. In what ways do I practice feel-good self-care?

2. In what ways do I practice the hard-but-good-for-me kinds of self-care?

3. In what ways do I practice avoidance masquerading as self-care?

4. Which of my self-care practices are likely to turn into avoidance behaviors?

5. What practices can I start to incorporate into my life to improve and expand my genuine self-care?

It Gets Harder Before It Gets Easier

Before you begin the work toward meeting and healing your anxiety, it's important to understand the role of exposure to anxiety-producing stimuli in this process. You can think of exposure as the opposite of avoidance. It is the practice of moving *toward* the thing that causes anxiety rather than away from it. Of course, practicing exposure often brings up painful emotions because it requires us to face what is making us anxious. However, the payoff is great. Each time we are exposed to our fears we become more desensitized to them and less anxious over time.

It is likely that during the course of this work you might question why you are being asked to lean into something that is painful, and especially why I encourage you to uncover old painful wounds that may have been the birthing place of your anxiety. It's only natural to ask this question, because often exposing yourself to the source of discomfort feels very counterproductive. Your anxiety voice will do everything in its power to convince you of this, because its main job is to identify and eliminate threats, preferably before they have even happened. In fact, I imagine it is possible that your anxiety voice is already screaming at you for reading this book and even thinking about doing this work. On the other hand, it could be that your logic knows you want to do this work—indeed, you *need* to do this work—so your anxiety is rather quiet at this time.

Regardless of how active your anxiety is now, there will surely be times throughout the course of this work when your anxiety raises its voice, persuading you to backpedal. This will be a convincing argument, because you've learned that the quickest way to avoid anxiety is to practice avoidance of the anxiety-producing stimuli. If the anxiety-producing stimuli is this work, it makes sense that your anxiety would do its best to persuade you to shove this book away in a bottom drawer, never to be revisited again.

As the many examples offered here have illustrated, avoiding this work will likely be effective in reducing anxiety in the short term; however, if you bought this book to get a better handle on your anxiety, then avoiding the work because it's uncomfortable will not be in accordance with your long-term values of creating and living a fulfilled, meaningful life. We must be willing to endure short-term discomfort for the long-term benefit of creating a values-driven life. Because of the likelihood that at some point you will question the productiveness of engaging in this work, the next exercise may be especially helpful now.

REFLECTION: What Is Your Why? A Journal Exercise

Reflect on the following questions and write your responses in your journal. You can revisit your answers at any time that your anxiety increases and you feel the urge to abandon the work.

- What arguments is my anxiety's voice likely to make while doing this work?

- In what ways will abandoning this work benefit me in the short term?

- In what ways will continuing with this work benefit me in the long term?

- What made me decide to purchase this book and engage in this work in the first place?

- How will I know when I need to take a break from this work because I need to do another, more immediately soothing kind of self-care?

- What are my values, and how does healing from anxiety fit in with them?

Note: There's a crucial distinction to be made between your anxiety's encouraging you to avoid this work because it is uncomfortable, and your body feeling unsafe while doing this work. In the former case, it may be appropriate to gently push through your anxiety to continue this work. In the latter, it's an indication that increased safety—and perhaps the oversight of a licensed therapist—is a necessary prerequisite to your continuing safely.

So how does exposure actually work? We discussed in chapter 1 that our survival brains are likely to draw a connection to a cause when we assess and respond to threats. For example, in scenario one, when my social anxiety gets the best of me and I cancel plans at the last minute, in the immediate rush of relief my anxiety voice will declare *I feel better because I skipped out on the party.*

The same concept applies when we practice exposure to the anxiety-producing stimuli. If, in scenario two, I face my anxiety head-on and attend the party, even if I have anxiety the entire time I'm at the party, I will likely feel that same relief when I am leaving the party *if attending was in line with my values.* In this instance, I might have the thought, *I feel really good because I was able to attend the party despite my anxiety, and I actually had a decent time.* The two outcomes here both result in my feeling good, and for both outcomes I draw causation. The first scenario left me thinking *I feel good because I avoided the party,* which is likely to be replaced with some unpleasant emotions over time; the second scenario leaves me thinking *I feel good because I attended the party.* The first scenario reinforces and strengthens the need to avoid parties in the future, whereas the second scenario reinforces and strengthens the need to push through my anxiety and attend parties in the future.

Our behavior choices are important because they always reinforce *something.* It becomes a matter of what we want to reinforce: anxiety and the limitations it imposes, or living freely.

When we pair an anxiety-producing stimulus with some degree of calmness, it begins to challenge our anxiety voice's argument that we need to avoid the anxiety-producing stimulus or else we will be in more danger. Let's revisit the chapter 1 scenario of healing from the traumatic dog bite in the park. When we revisit the place of the original trauma and practice the anxiety-regulation strategies outlined in chapter 2 to create the sensation of feeling calm, we begin to chip away at the narrative that the park is dangerous and start to increase the association between the park and feeling calm. It's like our anxiety voice says, *Wait a second. How is it that I can be in this park and feel relatively calm? Something is not adding up here.*

This contradictory experience is called *cognitive dissonance*. Cognitive dissonance happens whenever new information proves inconsistent with our previously held ideas about something. When you're doing this work, creating cognitive dissonance is an important indicator that your anxiety is starting to be challenged. The more times we expose ourselves to the original anxiety-producing stimulus and pair it with the sensation of feeling calm, the weaker the association between the stimulus and threat becomes, and our anxiety is replaced with neutral or pleasant emotions.

This behavioral association concept has been studied since the early 1900s. B. F. Skinner coined the term *operant conditioning* to describe the method of learning in which we are likely to either repeat or not repeat behaviors based on their positive or negative consequences. For example, a study was conducted in which lab rats pressed a lever when shown a green light and were rewarded with food. If they pressed the lever when the light was red, they were administered a mild electric shock. It did not take long for the rats to associate a red light with anxiety and press the lever only when the light was green. This is an adaptive response that helped keep them safe in this context. However, if the rats were moved to a different setting in which red lights caused the opposite result—a delivery of the food they were seeking—these rats would likely be in trouble because of the associations they had previously made.

Let's apply this concept to the scenario of being attacked by a dog in a park. Even if we had visited that park a hundred times before and it was always a pleasant or neutral environment, being attacked by a dog there just once is likely to be a strong enough consequence that we will begin to associate the park with fear in the future. Ideally, over time our logical brain would help us identify that the park is not actually dangerous; rather, that particular dog was. Then we would be able to return to the park with only mild anxiety, and the memory of the dog attack would not go on to cause problems in our lives.

If the traumatic memory of being attacked by a dog gets stuck and we do not integrate it properly as a single isolated incident, our brain may make other associations with the memory, and these will start to produce anxiety. Over time and with continued avoidance, we may become convinced that we need to avoid that park and dogs in general. This is how a past traumatic experience can start the cycle of avoidance and begin to cause more and more problems in our lives.

What Is Habituation, and How Does It Help?

So how do we prevent the cycle of avoidance from happening? Avoiding avoidance is the single most important thing we can do to stop anxiety in its tracks. In fact, exposure to the feared stimulus over time creates the opposite effect: *habituation*. Habituation refers to the decreasing of anxiety that happens when we are repeatedly exposed to the anxiety-producing stimulus. Each time we visit the park and are not attacked by a dog, the association between the park and being attacked becomes weaker. Over time, this means the park begins to cause us less and less anxiety, until going there becomes a neutral experience. If we can begin to pair the park with not only an absence of being attacked but also the presence of calm, pleasant emotions, we can begin to strengthen the association between the park and safety and enjoyment.

When anxiety does not fit the facts of the situation, there is a high likelihood that it developed as a result of some negative consequence you experienced at some point in your life, combined with repeated avoidance over time. The negative consequence can be real—like being made fun of—or only a perception, like assuming that people are silently judging you. When we continue to avoid the original anxiety-producing stimulus, we continue to reinforce the response of fear and anxiety. We cannot begin the process of habituation until we are willing to expose ourselves to the stimulus again.

For example, if my brain has paired social encounters with danger, the only way to extinguish this pairing is to attend social encounters while experiencing the absence of danger. If we avoid social encounters, we do not get this opportunity; instead, we reinforce the pairing of social encounters with danger, because we feel safer when we avoid them.

The same is true for my healing from anxiety while in professional meetings, which I mentioned in chapter 1. Although I did not avoid professional meetings, I did interpret ambiguous information during the meetings through the lens of *I am stupid*. For example, if I was not called on, or if, for an extended period after I had spoken, I sensed even the slightest bit of a chuckle from one of my superiors, I internalized that information as meaning that I was definitely stupid; as a result, strengthening the pairing in my mind between attending meetings and feeling threatened. Healing from this anxiety required me to expose myself to these kinds of encounters while feeling the absence of threat and instead a sense of safety. But because of the continuous pattern of pairing my meeting attendance with feeling stupid, my anxious voice had become so overpowering that it would not allow me to experience any amount of safety; instead, it would continuously alert me to the threat and implore me to avoid meetings altogether if I wanted to achieve safety. This cycle continued until my internship ended.

When Logic Isn't Enough

Getting caught in this cycle is usually an indicator that simply knowing these concepts isn't sufficient to break free of it. It's why logic-based solutions like "Just think calm thoughts" are unhelpful and invalidating. It's why I, a therapist with a master's degree in understanding these concepts, could not seem to wrangle my own anxiety.

Don't get me wrong: knowledge is power; it is important. Understanding from a scientific perspective how and why anxiety happens can help us comprehend the ways in which we are helping the problem and making it worse. It is an important starting place. But it is not enough. It is not the work. You can't logic your way out of an emotion—because emotions, by definition, are not logical. Healing from anxiety will require you to turn off your thinking brain and drop into your felt sense, your inner knowing, your intuition. This is not a skill that you have to cultivate; rather, it is an intrinsic strength that you can tap into. It has been there all along, pointing you in the opposite direction of your logic's roadmap. It is watching you struggle to climb the mountain of life while simultaneously being tethered to a boulder—the original little t trauma—where the consequence first happened.

In the next chapter, I will guide you through the process of pausing your ascent up the mountain of your life, tapping into your intuition, and turning around to tend to the boulders that are keeping you stuck. By doing so, you will untether yourself and begin to build a life in which all that energy you expend trying to dodge anxiety can instead be directed toward living in ways that are consistent with your values.

CHAPTER 4

befriending anxiety

By now you are likely thinking of your anxiety in a new way. You are probably making logical sense of what happened to make you anxious, and you are starting to understand how anxiety developed out of a need to protect you from something. You might have come to accept that your efforts to avoid anxiety usually fall short, and that healing from it is going to require turning toward it. You may even be thinking about how your cycle of anxiety perpetuates itself, and the common goal that you and your anxiety share. This new way of conceptualizing your anxiety is an important prerequisite to doing this work, but it is not the work itself.

The next few chapters will guide you through the main work required to heal your relationship with anxiety. You will start to experience your anxiety as separate from you, as a force with whom you can have a conversation. Then you will be encouraged (and equipped) to turn your logical or thinking brain off, allowing you to get a felt sense and deeper understanding of your anxiety, so that ultimately you can work with it to discover what is keeping you stuck.

It is important to remember that you and your anxiety are separate; it has its own thoughts, opinions, and voice, separate from yours. If it were one with you, you would never be in conflict with it. When you can give it space to share its perspective, when you listen to it nonjudgmentally, you will be much more effective at figuring it out than when you try to decide for it. This is similar to a situation when you are worried that you upset your friend in your most recent conversation. You can do some serious mental gymnastics trying to figure out whether you said or did something hurtful, but what's most effective is to go straight to the source of the information and ask her, "Did I hurt you?" The same is true for anxiety. It has a voice. It knows its perspective and doesn't want you to fill in the gaps about its wishes and needs without including it in the conversation. In the exercises that follow in this chapter, you will practice listening for the answers rather than using your logical brain to try to figure them out. Remember, anxiety, by definition, is not logical.

When Anxiety Doesn't Cooperate

Just because anxiety has its own voice doesn't mean it's going to be enthusiastic about communicating with you right off the bat. Remember when we talked about having decades-long qualms about your anxiety? It's important to consider this when working to establish a healthy relationship with it. Imagine being estranged from a family member for twenty years or more and then sitting down one day for coffee. In that first conversation, you might hold back a little. Or a lot. You might be angry. You might want to scream. You might have so much to say that you don't know how to say any of it. That first conversation could produce a myriad of responses depending on the relationship you had with this family member. Then fast forward to your tenth conversation with this family member: it will probably look and feel a lot different from your first.

The same is true for the conversations you will have with your anxiety. Even if your anxiety has been screaming at you for some time, you may find that it becomes challenging to access as you work through these exercises. Or you may find that it has so much to say that it becomes overwhelming to take it all in. Either of these experiences is okay, as is anything in the middle of these two ends of the spectrum. The more you listen to your anxiety and work to understand it, the more trust you will build, further repairing your relationship with it. Whatever the outcome of these exercises, as long as you are holding space for your anxiety rather than trying to extinguish, numb, or outrun it, you are doing right by it.

Remember that painful emotions do not mean you are backsliding. In fact, many times the opposite is true.

The exercises in this chapter are meant to be not a quick fix, but rather an ongoing practice. If you find your anxiety is completely inaccessible one day, that is okay. Tomorrow you can show up and try again. If you find that your anxiety is so overwhelming that you're unable to take in all of the information it's throwing at you, let it know that you hear it and that what it has to say is important to you; however, it is going to need to respect your limits for how much you can digest in one sitting. Keep in mind that on one day your anxiety might show up with very strong feelings toward you—exhaustion, anger, indignation—and may not be pleasant to communicate with. The very next day you might find your anxiety is happy to be acknowledged and enthusiastic about communicating with you. (Remember the analogy of the dysregulated four-year-old having a meltdown? It applies here.)

Repairing any relationship takes time, and your relationship with anxiety is no exception. Think of this work as a marathon, not a sprint. Check in with yourself and honor your pace. It is recommended that you give yourself ample time between exercises to allow yourself space to digest and synthesize the information you are gathering from your anxiety. Remember to honor your feelings too. You may have strong feelings about your anxiety that require time to sit with and process. Whatever you experience is okay. Stay with each exercise for as long as you need to in order to be able to gather the information that you need to answer the reflection questions. If at any time during this work you become overwhelmed, simply take note, ease up on this work, and return to some of the self-regulation exercises you practiced in chapter 2.

Meet Your Anxiety

The purpose of the first exercise is for you to consciously meet with your anxiety for the first time. In many ways, of course, you already have a relationship, though not the kind that serves you well. This time, rather than pushing your anxiety away or resisting it, you'll approach it with curiosity and without judgment. You will explore who it is and what it's like, and start to consider why it does what it does and what it wants. (You can also find an audio version to download in the online free tools at http://www.newharbinger.com/48756)

EXERCISE: Consciously Connecting with Your Anxiety

Find a place in your home or office that is free of distractions, and take a comfortable seated position. Notice the surface that you are on; feel the weight of gravity grounding your body to the floor or chair. Pay attention to the way the structure that you're sitting or lying on supports you. Close your eyes and take a couple of full, easy, centering breaths.

Turn your attention inward, and just see what you notice. Perhaps you notice stray thoughts coming into your mind. You might be thinking *What is going to happen if I connect with my anxiety?* or *I'm not sure if this is going to work.* Maybe you're thinking about what to make for dinner tonight. Just notice. Take note of any physical sensations or emotions bubbling up to the surface. Perhaps you feel doubt, fear, anxiety. Maybe you feel somewhat blank. You might experience strong physical sensations like a headache or restless legs, or maybe your body feels calm and light. Just keep noticing without trying to do or change anything.

Now, see if you can connect with the part of you that feels anxious. You might find it easier to connect to a physical manifestation of anxiety, or perhaps an emotional one. Whatever ways your anxiety manifests right now, approach it with curiosity. Maybe you connect to it right away, or maybe it's aloof. Just notice this, not trying to change it.

See if you can identify where the anxiety is showing up in your body. This might come to you immediately, or maybe you can't seem to place it. It might feel like a small part of you in a specific location, or perhaps it feels like a surge of electricity coursing throughout your entire body.

Take note of whether your anxiety is moving in your body or staying in one position.

Notice its form—does it feel like a solid, liquid, or gas?

See if you can give your anxiety a color and a shape. Maybe it's many colors all jumbled together. Maybe it's scribble lines. Maybe it's a sharp object. Maybe it's a heavy weight. However it's showing up, see if you can acknowledge it as separate from you.

Continue to notice it without judgment. Maintain an intention of learning about it rather than fixing it. Sit with it for a few minutes. See if it can acknowledge your presence. Ask it to notice that, perhaps for the first time, you're not trying to smother it.

Once you've taken in all of the information you can about your anxiety, thank it for showing up today. Let it know that this is the start of a new relationship with it, and you're looking forward to getting to know it better. If it didn't show up today, acknowledge that and let it know that you'll revisit it again later.

With the experience fresh in your mind, take out your journal and answer these reflection questions.

1. How easy or difficult did it feel to connect with your anxiety?

2. Could you see your anxiety? Feel it? Both?

3. What did you notice about your anxiety? Did it have a color or shape?

4. Did your anxiety move during the exercise or stay in the same location?

5. How old did your anxiety feel?

6. How did you feel toward your anxiety?

7. How did this anxiety feel toward you? How did it feel about being explored?

8. How did you know that this anxiety was separate from you?

9. What else, if anything, did you notice about the experience of trying to meet your anxiety without judgment?

It's likely that something about this exercise surprised you. Just as we can't anticipate how we are going to feel after meeting an estranged family member of twenty-plus years for the first time, we can't know what reactions we might experience when going inside and connecting with anxiety in this way for the first time. I want you to remember something that's more important than the outcome of this exercise: that you have made the very real effort to stop running and start facing your anxiety, and that in itself is a huge step to be acknowledged!

Now let's unpack what came up for you during this exercise.

Building Trust

There is a lot of information that comes from how easy or challenging it was to connect with your anxiety. If it was challenging, that might tell you that your anxiety is somewhat distant and has a hard time trusting you. Imagine if you were invited to meet your estranged family member and you decided to no-show to the meeting. This ghosting behavior would probably be an indicator that you didn't feel emotionally ready to face this person or you didn't trust their intentions. The same is true for your anxiety; if it no-showed you, it's likely that it, or another part of you, feels apprehensive in some way about your connecting with your anxiety. Perhaps it doesn't trust your intentions. Perhaps it doesn't believe this exercise will work. Perhaps it fears that if you fully feel the emotion, you'll never be able to make it stop. If this is the case, it doesn't mean that your anxiety will never come around (after all, it's had no problem showing up before!); it just means that it's going to take some extra time to establish trust before it shows up for you in this context. The more you connect with it, the more trust will be established.

If you experienced the opposite and your anxiety was overwhelmingly present, it may be an indicator that it's been feeling silenced for a long time, and now it's working in overdrive to try and protect you. That is good information to have, and in the next exercise you will gain more insight into what it's working so hard to protect you from. You can also let it know that you understand it has a lot to say, but that you're going to need to work together on how much information it throws at you in one sitting. Remember, you share a common goal: It wants to be heard, and you want to hear it. So if you need it to scale back some in order to be able to hear it, it should be open to the compromise.

One strategy for lessening the overwhelming feelings you may experience when connecting to your anxiety is to imagine a barrier between you and your anxiety. Perhaps it's a brick wall with you on one side and your anxiety on the other side. You can imagine talking to it through a hole in the wall. Another strategy is to imagine talking to your anxiety on a screen, perhaps FaceTime, on which it appears in a small picture at a lower corner of your smartphone. Both of these exercises can help reduce the threat of being totally overtaken by anxiety.

In addition to noting the accessibility of your anxiety, it's important to take note of how old your anxiety feels, as well as how you feel toward each other. It's very common for your anxiety to feel younger than your actual age, because it usually presents as the age it was when it starting doing its job. For example, if your anxiety developed due to a little t trauma when you were eight years old, anxiety might feel eight years old too, because that's the memory it's responding to. Remember, anxiety that doesn't fit the facts of the situation is responding to a past threat as if it were a current threat. For example, when I had anxiety in my professional internship meetings, it was actually responding to the experience I had at age five of being laughed at during a family dinner. It makes good sense, then, that when I first met my anxiety, it felt like a five-year-old. If your anxiety does feel childlike, this can make it easier to develop compassion for it. You likely wouldn't tell a five-year-old to shut up and go away, and if your anxiety feels like it's five years old, you can treat it with the same patience and understanding you would have for any other five-year-old.

There are also benefits to your anxiety's feeling the same age or close in age to you. This means that while seemingly irrational, your anxiety has the logic and communication skills of an adult. An adult can be a little easier to reason, compromise, and settle disputes with than a child is, because an adult has the ability to think critically and see both sides of an argument. Having anxiety that feels similar in age to your own age may also indicate that your anxiety is responding to a little t trauma that happened more recently, which can sometimes make it easier to heal from because it doesn't have many years of being reinforced.

It's important to take note of how you felt toward your anxiety during this exercise and how it felt toward you. As you do this work, it's equally important to monitor how this shifts over time, as it likely will. The ultimate goal is to achieve mutual compassion for one another; however, be aware that often takes time to achieve. It makes sense for anxiety to lack trust in you or to feel any other emotion that an ignored person might feel. Similarly, it is common for you to feel fearful of your anxiety, particularly about its working too hard and causing more problems in your life. It also makes sense to feel annoyed or angry at your anxiety because of how it's impeded you in life. Over time, the goal is to be able to hash out your qualms with it and arrive at a place of compassion for the job it's doing, but it's important to honor the feelings that are showing up now because they are equally valid.

You Are Not Your Anxiety

The most important takeaway from this exercise is the ability to experience anxiety as separate from you, with a separate name and visual representation from yourself. Maybe you imagine it as an orange triangle, or maybe you think of the character Fear from the movie *Inside Out*. It doesn't matter so much what name and image you assign to it, but it's important to start thinking about it as a separate force. Before starting this work, you likely experienced anxiety as all-consuming. You might have had thoughts like *I'm anxious* or *I can't do that because of my anxiety* and labeled yourself as an anxious person. When we are fused with our anxiety, we become something we hate. *If I am anxious and I hate anxiety, then I hate myself.* This way of thinking about anxiety and oneself leads to secondary emotions such as shame, which can start to cause an entirely different set of problems. In reality, you existed before your anxiety. It is not you. It is a part of you that has a job to do, and you likely have many other parts of you that do different jobs.

If you need some convincing of this, think of all of the things about you that have nothing to do with anxiety. Perhaps you are an aunt who loves your nieces and nephews; maybe you like to cook; maybe you are a great writer, or a great friend. When you can experience your anxiety as separate from you, it opens up the opportunity for some really important dialogue. You can then work to understand it and befriend it, and you can work with it toward achieving your common goal. If there is one lasting skill that I hope you glean from these exercises, it is the ability to see your anxiety as separate from yourself.

Going Deeper

Once you have a felt sense of the who and what of your anxiety, the next step is to explore the when, where, and whys—when it shows up, where it shows up, and why it's showing up. The following exercise is designed to give you these insights into your own cycle of anxiety, in addition to the job it's doing for you. Remember to approach this exercise with the same open mind that you brought to the first one, and with the understanding that your anxiety may show up similarly, or perhaps completely differently from your first contact with it. Honor your limits, and take breaks as needed. Remember, this is a marathon, not a sprint. (You can also find an audio version of this exercise to download in the online free tools at http://www.newharbinger.com/48756.)

EXERCISE: Deepening Your Understanding of Your Anxiety

Find a place in your home or office that is free of distractions. In a comfortable seated position, close your eyes if it's comfortable for you, and take a couple of deep inhales, noticing the full course of each breath: the inhale, the pause at the top of the breath before the exhale, the exhale, and the pause before the next inhale.

Turn your attention inside, and see what you notice. Perhaps you notice various thoughts, emotions, and body sensations. Take note of what's there, acknowledging everything that's showing up. Try to maintain a perspective of curiosity rather than a judgmental one.

Now see if you can connect with the part of you that experiences anxiety. Let it know that you're here to check back in with it, rather than blocking it or trying to get it to go away. Once you are able to connect with it, see what you notice about it. How is it showing up today? Does it have the same color, shape, identity, or age as it did it in the previous exercise? Where is it in relation to you? Closer or farther away than previously? Is it moving or static? Does it have a larger presence than it did in the first exercise, or is it smaller and/or more quiet? Take in as much information as you can about it.

Next, let your anxiety know that you're here to learn more about it. Thank it for the information it has shared with you thus far, and then, when it feels right, ask your anxiety what goal it has for you. Tell it that you know it's doing an important job, and you want to understand more about that job it's doing for you. Don't respond just yet. Just listen.

Perhaps you can ask it what it's working to protect you from.

Ask it what it fears.

Ask it how it's helping you. Listen for the answer rather than trying to figure it out. See if you can listen with compassion.

Ask it when it feels most threatened.

Ask it when it feels like it needs to work the hardest.

See if you can acknowledge the importance of its job. Tell it that while you may not agree on how best to get that job done, you share a mutual goal.

Ask if there are ever times when it feels like it doesn't have to work so hard.

Ask what makes it feel soothed.

Let your anxiety know that without trying to change it, you'd like to see if it can acknowledge the problems that it's caused in your life.

Try to get a felt sense of what anxiety's goal is and the job it's doing. Try to understand when it works the hardest, and when it gets a break.

Acknowledge its effort. If it feels right, thank it.

Ask it if it has anything else it wants to share with you now.

Once you've taken in all of the information you can about your anxiety, thank it for showing up today. Let it know that you are working hard to try and understand it, and you're looking forward to continuing to learn about its role. If it didn't show up today, acknowledge that and let it know that you'll revisit it again later.

With the experience fresh in your mind, take out your journal and answer these reflection questions.

1. How challenging or easy was it to connect to your anxiety today? Did it feel more or less accessible than last time?

2. Could you see your anxiety? Feel it? Both?

3. What did you notice about your anxiety? Did it have a color or shape?

4. How did you feel toward your anxiety today? Did this differ from last time you explored it?

5. How did your anxiety feel toward you today? Was it more or less open to communicating with you?

6. Where did your anxiety show up today? Was it closer in proximity to you than last time? Further away? Did it move during your time together?

7. What did you learn about anxiety's goal for you?

8. When does your anxiety work the hardest?

9. When is your anxiety most calm and soothed? When does it get a break?

10. What is it working to protect you from? What are its fears?

11. In what ways is it trying to help you?

12. Were you able to acknowledge that you share a common goal with your anxiety? Could it acknowledge how it's caused problems in your life?

13. What else did you notice about your anxiety?

These exercises can and should be used as a tool for reflection anytime you experience anxiety that does not fit the facts of the situation you are in. When anxiety shows up, the initial impulse is usually to extinguish it as quickly as possible. If you can learn to turn toward your anxiety with curiosity sooner after you experience it, you will spend less time and energy fighting it.

As you continue to move through these exercises, it's important to take note of any shifts in how you experience your anxiety. Hopefully, as you continue this work your anxiety will feel more easily accessible, closer in proximity to you, more trusting and easier to talk to. Any shifts you notice, whether you perceive them as positive or negative, are usually indicative of progress. Returning to the example of your estranged family member, if you no-showed the first scheduled meeting but showed up to the second and got angry, that would show forward movement even if it felt more painful to yell and scream than it did to no-show. Movement in any direction is progress. Of course, if your anxiety initially shows up with a hostile presentation and over time becomes more calm and easy to talk to, this is an indication that it is likely experiencing increased trust and safety in its relationship with you. No matter what shifts might happen, it's important to notice them.

Your Anxiety Wants the Best for You

Perhaps the most important information you will gather from these encounters with your anxiety is a better understanding of the job it's doing. We know that anxiety usually develops from a wound, and it is working to protect you from reexperiencing that wound. While no two experiences of anxiety are the same, there are some common themes that emerge in the types of jobs anxiety usually takes on. Many times this understanding does not come easily, but rather requires many conversations and reflections. Anxiety might not even be totally clear on its job (especially if it's presenting as a five-year-old!), and if it isn't really sure, it's going to have a hard time communicating it to you clearly. Patience is really important here. With patience and continuing effort, you and your anxiety can work together to come to a mutual understanding. A helpful question you might ask yourself when working to uncover the threat that anxiety is protecting you from is *If this bad thing happens, what does it say about me as a person?*

Often anxiety is working to protect you from rejection of some sort. This was certainly the case for me when I kept experiencing anxiety related to looking or sounding dumb in my professional work environment. I didn't always know that I feared rejection, however; I just knew that I didn't want to sound dumb. In doing this work, I was able to collaborate with my anxiety on what exactly the threat was, and I realized I was sure that if I sounded dumb, I was going to be laughed at. It followed that if I am laughed at, that means I won't be respected. If I'm not respected, I am rejected. If I am rejected, I am unworthy. As soon as I uncovered this fear, it made perfect sense why my anxiety was working so hard. To my anxiety, my worth as a human was at stake.

Other times, anxiety might be working to protect you from failure. This kind of anxiety might show up when you are goal-setting, future planning, or taking forward steps that feel in line with your personal or professional growth. Other threats that anxiety often responds to are a sense of being out of control, being unsafe, feeling defective, or being responsible for something bad happening.

Once you understand the main threat that your anxiety is responding to, you will likely get a better grasp on when it is most likely to show up. For example, if you identify that your anxiety fears being out of control, you will start to notice that it works harder whenever your sense of control is threatened. Similarly, if your anxiety seems to strike unexpectedly, you may be able to better pinpoint the trigger for your anxiety by asking yourself, *In what ways am I feeling out of control right now?* This is important for many reasons:

- It affirms that your anxiety is separate from you.

- It acknowledges that your anxiety is working hard at its job.

- It allows you to acknowledge that you share a common goal of feeling in control of your life and adopting some compassion toward it.

- It will eventually give you the opportunity to ask your anxiety to ease up some and trust that you can take it from here.

When these steps become part of your response to anxiety, major transformation happens.

What Do You Need from Anxiety?

The last step in this piece of the work is to acknowledge how your anxiety has hindered your life. This relationship is a two-way street, and while you are working very hard to understand and develop compassion for your anxiety, it's equally important that your anxiety considers your needs and perspective as well. While you can acknowledge that it's doing a really important job, you can also ask it to acknowledge that the way it's been doing that job has been less than helpful. Facilitating this conversation can feel threatening to your anxiety, just as it might feel threatening to you if a friend came to you to tell you how your presence has been causing problems in their life. Defensiveness is bound to come up, and that's okay. Remember that any shifts in experience are likely indicative of forward movement.

It's important to let your anxiety know that you're not trying to get it to go away; in fact, quite the opposite. However, you would like it to see that when it works as hard as it does, there are consequences. Maybe you shy away from participating in social gatherings for fear of anything negative that might happen. Perhaps when things seem to be going "too well" in a new intimate relationship, your anxiety about being emotionally vulnerable causes you to sabotage the relationship so you can't end up getting hurt. Or maybe you hold yourself back from achieving your goals because it's more comfortable to stay put. Once your anxiety can acknowledge that there might be a better way to respond to these perceived threats—a way that cause less negative impact in your life—and you can work with it to find this balance, the gates to healing swing open.

Preparing to Work with Stuck Memories

Now that you have consciously connected with your anxiety, developed curiosity and compassion for it, and have a better understanding of the job it is doing, you can prepare to work with it to uncover stuck memories.

We'll spend the next pages—and some hours of your time—practicing some of the skills that will help you uncover and unstick stuck memories. You will increase your skill at getting quiet and turning your attention from external stimuli to your inner world. When you live with anxiety, learning to do this can be tricky. You have probably gotten very good at tuning out your inner experience, since it is so uncomfortable. You might notice that you are often caught up in what is going on in the world around you, investing emotional energy in other people's problems more easily than you can sit with your own emotional experiences. It may seem counterintuitive to actually turn your attention within, where the anxiety lives.

Another obstacle that some people face when learning to go inside and work with their stuck memories is feeling blocked from doing so. In this context, I'm not talking about being blocked by external forces like a busy schedule or chaotic household. I'm referring to feeling blocked from the inside, like you want to go there but there is a protective force inside that won't allow you to.

This can be an indicator that there is another part of you that feels threatened by doing this work. Just as anxiety may be trying to protect you from embarrassment, shame, or some other emotion, there can be a part of you that develops to protect you from anxiety. Or it could mean that a part of you believes it needs to protect you from accessing this memory because it will be too overwhelming to process. Remember that we are hardwired to avoid pain. Leaning into painful past memories in this way is counterintuitive, so patience is key. Trust that your body and brain are working hard to keep you safe. With a little reassurance from you, combined with being shown that this work actually is not dangerous after all, over time a beautiful working relationship between you and your anxiety can and will unfold.

If you experience this blocked sensation when you try to go inside, you will need to spend some time with the part of you that feels resistant to exploring these memories. Ask it how it's trying to help you, what it fears, and what it would need from you in order to feel safe to explore your inner world in this way. If you learned early on in your life that emotions are not safe to experience, and as a result you have spent the rest of your life pushing them away, breaking through this barrier will take several conversations with your anxiety. You might ask your anxiety the following questions to facilitate this unblocking:

- What do you need in order to feel safe accessing this memory?

- If we do explore these past memories and it becomes too overwhelming, how will we know that we need to back out?

- What exercises from chapter 2 can we practice to help reorient to the present and feel safe again?

- What is the benefit of doing this work (our why)?

Again, patience is key. You might make an agreement with the part of you that is blocking you from these memories to explore your inner world in very small doses, perhaps thirty seconds at a time, so that it remains a safe experience. Or you might imagine looking at the memory as if it was on a TV screen rather than in real life, so the sensory experience is less vivid. Or you could imagine a wall between you and the memory, so that it is accessible yet there is a barrier between you and the memory, keeping you safe from it.

If after exploring this for several sittings you still feel blocked, it may mean that the memory is not in fact a little t trauma but rather a *big t trauma* that needs the support of a licensed therapist to help you process it. If you attempt to charge ahead into these memories before it feels safe for all parts to do so, it is likely you will continue to feel more and more blocked. The goal is not for it to feel totally comfortable to go inside and explore your anxiety (after all, the point is to experience and lean into some discomfort), but it does need to feel accessible. You will know it is accessible if you can revisit it while remaining in your healing window of tolerance; that is, the memory comes to mind, you can experience some sensory information that it contains (images, sounds, emotions), and you can do so without experiencing hypo- or hyperarousal. Refer back to the image of the window of tolerance in chapter 2 to use as a guide.

Once you are able to turn your attention inward, you must then be able to notice and experience your anxiety as a force separate from you that can guide you through your past experiences. If you can notice your anxiety and experience it as an energy separate from your adult, logical self, you can allow it to successfully show you what it needs to without becoming completely immersed in the experience.

Remember the concept of dual awareness? When I work with my clients, I ask them to achieve this by imagining having one foot in the present (in the therapy room with me) while having one foot in the past, exploring past trauma memories. This way, they always have an anchor to safety—right here, right now, with me, where there is no danger.

Throughout the trauma work, I will often ask them to pause, take a break, and notice their present surroundings where it is safe. This helps them remain in their healing zone.

It may be helpful for you, too, to find some kind of safety anchor in the present while diving into past memories. That can be anything that feels calming in your environment: a pet, an essential oil, a picture of you and a loved one. When going back into past experiences, imagine having one foot in the past experience while also remaining in the present where it is safe. Your safety anchor can be a helpful reminder that you are revisiting a memory, not reliving it.

The last prerequisite to working with your anxiety in this way is establishing trust between you and your anxiety. You have to trust that anxiety is working hard to protect you from something and to have some compassion for the job it's doing, even though it inconveniences you. Your anxiety has to trust that you are a safe adult who can help it not have to work so hard, rather than trying to extinguish it (as you probably have been trying to do for some time!).

If you feel angry, contentious, or resentful of your anxiety, it is likely that you could benefit from establishing more trust prior to exploring stuck memories. Your anxiety is going to be your tour guide into these memories, and the more you can trust it to guide you, the more collaborative and successful an experience you will have. Once you can adopt a curious and compassionate stance toward your anxiety and can trust that it has valuable information for you to see, you are likely ready to move forward.

At this point, you are likely starting to see your anxiety as a force separate from you with whom you can have a conversation. If you have not yet been able to have a dialogue with your anxiety, it's important to stick with the exercises in this chapter before moving on.

This chapter has taught you skills and practices for exploring your inner experience without becoming blocked; to see your anxiety as separate from you; and to develop a mutually trusting relationship with your anxiety. These skills prepare you to allow your anxiety to guide you into your past experiences to show you where it is stuck. The newfound trust you have established in your relationship with your anxiety will be the force that allows it to guide you through your past experiences safely and to help you uncover and untether from the boulders keeping you stuck, so that your past experiences no longer have to dictate your current emotions. Setting forth on that guiding relationship is what the following chapter is all about.

CHAPTER 5

welcoming anxiety as your guide

In the last chapter, you learned to experience your anxiety as a separate entity with its own motives—and one with which you can have a conscious relationship. In this chapter you'll learn to go inside, trusting your anxiety enough to allow it to show you the boulders or little t traumas that are keeping your anxiety active and you feeling stuck. If you haven't yet been able to have a dialogue with your anxiety, you should spend some more time on the practices in chapter 4, establishing a more curious, conscious relationship with your anxiety. Here, you'll begin to see how that work can transform your life.

The work you do in this chapter will equip you with all of the tools needed to heal your relationship with your anxiety. You will, perhaps for the first time, let go of trying to suppress anxiety symptoms and will instead uncover the source of your anxiety. Now that you have been able to connect with your anxiety and adopt curiosity and compassion toward it, you can allow your anxiety to guide you into your past experiences and show you where you are tethered.

In this chapter you will ask your anxiety to share with you its most fundamental fear, and from there you will participate in a float back exercise that will help you identify where this fear originated. Next, with your anxiety as your guide, you will create a timeline of little t trauma events that are the boulders keeping you stuck. This will become your roadmap for untethering from these boulders. You will then create an adaptive timeline of events that will highlight past experiences that support what your logic knows to be true (that is, *I am good enough*). This timeline will provide evidence to the contrary of your anxiety's fears, and serve as a logical anchor as you begin the untethering.

Must You Go Back There?

If you are wondering if it's really necessary to go back to past little t trauma experiences in order to heal from anxiety, you're not alone. When I ask a new client, "What prompted you to seek therapy at this time in your life?" I usually do not hear "I want to revisit the way my mother treated me when I was a kid" or "I'd like to dive into my past emotionally abusive relationship with my ex-boyfriend." Most people talk about symptoms they are currently experiencing that they want relief from. My clients Sara and Meg (names and some details changed) are good examples of this.

Sara had lived almost her whole life with high anxiety about exposure to blood. On a couple of occasions she had found herself unable to do things that were very important to her because of her anxiety. Sara was an ally of the LGBTQ+ community, and after the 2016 Pulse nightclub shooting she wanted to be able to donate blood to help the survivors who were in desperate need. Despite her strong desire to help in this way, her anxiety made it impossible. Not long after this, Sara witnessed a motor vehicle accident and felt a strong urge to pull over and render aid. But she couldn't bear the thought of seeing people injured and bleeding.

Sara came to therapy wanting to address her blood phobia because, as just described, it had started to interfere with her ability to live according to her values. She did not come to therapy saying, "I want to address my traumatic childhood experiences with blood." It wasn't until we started doing the work that Sara acknowledged that we needed to address her first traumatic experience with blood at age eleven, when her dad was badly injured and she feared the worst.

Similarly, Meg came to therapy to address her social anxiety, as it had recently prevented her from doing what she had long dreamed of: rushing for a sorority. She had such a strong fear of rejection that she couldn't bear the thought of participating in rush week and not matching with any sororities. So instead, she did not participate at all. When this left her feeling depressed and isolated after seeing all of her friends match, she sought therapy.

In Meg's first therapy session, she said she wanted to address her feelings of depression and anxiety. We explored where her anxiety and depression stemmed from and discovered an underlying fear of rejection, which Meg had not yet been consciously aware of. After doing this work together for some time, we discovered that in the sixth grade Meg had experienced an unresolved little t trauma, in which a group of girls announced that they no longer wanted to be friends with Meg. This rejection had devastated her. I was not surprised that Meg had not come to therapy saying she would like to address this experience of bullying that happened to her in sixth grade. She had come because she wanted to stop feeling so depressed and anxious *right now*. For her to do that, we needed to look at what purpose anxiety was serving for her. As it turned out, it was working hard to prevent her from ever again feeling the way she had in sixth grade. Once we discovered this, she was able to heal that wound and change her relationship with anxiety.

Again, you are probably not reading this book because you cannot wait to dive into the painful things that have happened in your past. It is more likely that you are reading this book because you want to get a handle on your anxiety in the present. But to get you there, we must explore what past trauma the anxiety is protecting you from.

How Trauma Memories Get Stuck

Francine Shapiro developed the adaptive information processing (AIP) model to describe why and how past trauma memories get stuck and cause problems later in life. According to Solomon and Shapiro (2008), our brains assimilate new experiences into already existing memory networks. You can think of a memory network as a web of experiences that are connected in your brain by related images, thoughts, emotions, or body sensations. And you can think of your trauma timeline as one particular memory network, and your adaptive timeline as a different memory network. Each memory network contains various experiences that are grouped together in your brain based on the common way they made you feel about yourself, others, or the world.

These memory networks are the basis for our perceptions, attitudes, and behaviors. When this process is working supportively, the new information we take in connects and integrates with our existing memory network, allowing us to make sense of it with no problems. For example, when I have a random and delightful encounter with a nice dog at the park, the sensory information will connect to previous pleasant experiences I have had with dogs and integrate smoothly into that memory network (*dogs are great*) and without inner conflict. But if I have a traumatic experience with a dog at a park, this experience and the new idea that comes with it—*dogs can be dangerous*—creates inner conflict because it does not fit with what I previously knew to be true about dogs.

Shapiro's AIP model explains that an experience that is particularly distressing or traumatic may create its own memory network when it is unable to connect with other memory networks that hold helpful, true information. This can happen when we have an experience that is overwhelming to our nervous system because it is in direct conflict with a belief we previously held about ourself, others, or the world. When this happens, we can't make sense of the new information, given the way we understand the world.

For example, let's say I'm studying for an important exam, and I hold a memory network full of past experiences of doing very well on exams. I may believe that I'm a smart and capable person. If I study as hard as I always have in the past but end up failing the exam, I will need to find a way to make sense of this. Ideally, I will make sense of this in a way that allows me to maintain the idea that I am smart and capable. That is, this memory will integrate into my existing memory network seamlessly. Perhaps I will come to the conclusion that I failed the exam not because I am not smart, but because I didn't get any sleep the night before, which compromised my powers of concentration and recall on exam day. Once integrated, this memory becomes an exception to the rule and is not likely to cause ongoing problems in my life.

When we can't make sense of memories in a way that integrates them into our existing memory network, the memories can get stuck in their own network and become boulders that we get tethered to. If I cannot find another way to make sense of failing the exam, this will challenge my belief that I am smart and capable. If this experience cannot integrate, and I make sense of it by thinking I am not as smart and capable as I once thought, it will form its own memory network and carry with it the belief that I'm actually incompetent. This creates a feeling of disconnection between what my logic knows to be true and what actually feels true. I may have the experience of logically *knowing* I am smart and capable, but *feeling* like I'm actually an imposter. There is an inner conflict when we have separate memory networks holding conflicting ideas, creating a stuck feeling.

This stuckness is what occurred for me as a result of the way my dinner table memory of being laughed at was integrated into my memory network. Prior to this experience at age five, I had likely had several experiences that had taught me I was capable and smart. For example, when I took my first steps, learned the alphabet, or created anything artistic, I was applauded and told some version of "Wow! Great job!" This started to develop the memory network of adaptive information that said that I was adequate.

Later in life, I had experiences that suggested that I was smart and capable, like when I got a 4.0 GPA in college, when I landed a really competitive internship, and that time when my graduate school classmate referred to me as "the smartest girl I know." I would have told you that logically I knew I probably wasn't stupid, but in those internship meetings when I was called on to speak and trembled with fear, it certainly did not feel true. And knowing logically that I was smart had almost no impact on the anxiety I felt associated with sounding dumb.

According to the AIP model, this disconnect between what I logically knew to be true and what felt true happened because the experience I'd had at the dinner table at five was existing in a different, isolated memory network that carried with it the belief that I am stupid. The memory networks were not integrated; they existed separately and were not communicating with one another. When this disconnect happens, we can assume the memory that is stuck in its own memory network is either a little t or a big t trauma.

Not Every Distressing Experience Is Traumatic

You might be wondering, *Does every upsetting experience cause trauma, then?* The answer is no. We take in tons of sensory information all day long, a lot of which conflicts with our preexisting beliefs. Not all distressing events will be stored in their own memory networks. We can have an experience that conflicts with existing information in our memory network and still integrate the memory without consequence. When our brains do this successfully, even a very scary memory will not be stored as a trauma memory.

For example, if I'm bitten by a dog but hold a preexisting belief that dogs are wonderful, trustworthy creatures, this attack may cause inner conflict, but I can still successfully integrate the memory into an existing network without its getting stuck. I might make sense of this experience by adopting the belief that, generally speaking, dogs are safe and wonderful; however, there are times when a particular dog feels threatened that may cause it to act out aggressively. I may think that I was bitten because I carelessly reached down to pet the dog without allowing it time to sniff my hand and give me permission. This allows the memory to integrate into my current memory network without getting stuck and causing problems later.

Distressing memories will integrate into an existing memory network based on the meaning we assign to them. This is why you could have one experience in your past that would be universally labeled as traumatic, like a near-death experience, but not require specific therapeutic intervention or cause any problems later in your life. Meanwhile, something like being rejected in sixth grade, which others might see as a normal, everyday childhood experience, can cause crippling social anxiety into adulthood.

Because of the significance of the thoughts we have about our experiences, two people can experience the exact same traumatic event together, and one might integrate it successfully while the other goes on to develop posttraumatic stress from it. For example, several years ago, when I was driving in my car with my friend as a passenger, we got into a car accident. I was distracted while driving, and the accident was my fault. Both my friend and I experienced the same sensory event—hearing the screeching of the tires and the crunching of the metal on my car. We both felt the same impact of the collision and had similar injuries from it. While both of us experienced a lot of fear and stress from the incident, my friend was able to make sense of it and integrate it into her memory without its causing later problems. She had the thought that car accidents happen often; she will learn from this event, and in the future when she is the driver she will take extra precautions to ensure she is very alert, which may prevent accidents and keep her safe. On the other hand, I walked away from the accident thinking that my negligence had put someone else's life at risk, which meant I was a bad person. This memory got stored in its own memory network because it could not coexist among my other memories that suggested the opposite. The same distressing event was stored traumatically for me, but was only temporarily distressing for my friend, based on our different beliefs about the event.

According to the AIP theory, when an experience is stored in its own dysfunctional memory network, the memory becomes frozen in time and can be retriggered when we experience sensory information similar to the original event. This information can include images, thoughts, emotions, or body sensations. When we experience an emotional reaction that feels disproportionate to the facts of our current situation, it is likely a result of an unresolved past event becoming reactivated.

How Can You Know if You Need to Revisit a Memory?

A good indicator that you are experiencing a disconnect between memory networks is when you know something to be true about yourself, other people, or the world, yet in certain situations the opposite *feels* true. In my work as a therapist, my clients often remark that what they *know* to be true is not connecting to what *feels* true, and they are puzzled by how this can be. Shapiro's AIP theory suggests that this points to an experience or experiences that are frozen and cannot integrate into a memory network. In this case, the frozen experience is causing the feeling, while your existing memory network is what your logic knows to be true. When this disconnect exists, we have to revisit the experience that is frozen and help it get unfrozen. There are many therapeutic modalities that offer different approaches and interventions for how best to accomplish this. For our purposes here, I hope to teach you to rely on the part of you that is trying to alert you to danger (your anxiety) to be your guide into your past experiences. It can show you where you are stuck and give you a route to healing.

The following exercise will invite you to connect to your anxiety and allow it to guide you into your past experiences to start gaining an understanding of the boulders keeping you stuck. (You can also find an audio version of this exercise to download in the online free tools at http://www.newharbinger.com/48756.)

EXERCISE: Exploring Fear

Find a place in your home or office that is free of distractions. In a comfortable seated position, take a couple of deep breaths into your diaphragm as you close your eyes and turn your attention inward. Start by noticing the sensation of your breath entering your nostrils, moving into your lungs, and then exiting from your nostrils or mouth. Stay here, noticing your breathing, for as long as it feels right.

Next, see if you can connect with the part of you that feels anxious. Perhaps its presence is obvious and you notice it immediately. Maybe you feel calm right now and the anxious part of you is more distant and difficult to connect to. Don't force anything to happen; just be still and notice what's going on inside. Let any stray thoughts pass by like clouds in the sky. If you have trouble connecting to your anxiety, bring up a recent experience in which you felt anxious. Do your best to feel into that experience. As you revisit this experience, notice if the part of you that holds anxiety becomes more noticeable. Again, don't force anything to happen. If it is still not showing up, perhaps it is not the right time or place; you can try again another time.

Once you do connect with your anxiety, notice where it is located in your body. Take note of its size and shape. If it had a color, what would it be? Perhaps it takes the form of an inanimate object, or perhaps it feels like a childlike part of you. However it is showing up, acknowledge its separateness from you. See if you can notice where it is in proximity to you. Perhaps it is a younger version of you sitting or standing right next to you, or maybe it's farther away. Notice the energy between the two of you. How do you feel toward it? Perhaps there is tension or reluctance or distrust. Perhaps there's a compassionate, loving energy.

As you sit with this part of you, see if you can engage a little more curiously or compassionately. See if you can let go of any judgment, so you can see your anxiety more clearly.

Once you feel mutual compassion and curiosity, ask your anxiety to show you its biggest fear. Turn your thinking brain off and just listen. This part of you has the answers that you seek, but you cannot access them by figuring them out; you must listen for them. Approach your anxiety as you would approach your most beloved friend who is sharing with you their most vulnerable truth. Be curious.

Allow anxiety to show you what it fears. Maybe it will show you a visual scenario that feels very familiar to you. Perhaps it will blurt out its fear using words. However it communicates with you, stay with it and stay curious.

Give your anxiety as much time and space as it needs. It may take some time to sort through all of the fears it wants to show you. Be patient. Continue to breathe. Once you have a sense of what your anxiety fears, sit with it for a minute. Can you notice how important this is to your anxiety? Can you see how hard it has been working to prevent this from happening? Even if this doesn't make logical sense just yet, acknowledge the fear. It is very real to your anxiety. Practice validating your anxiety as you would validate a scared child.

Once you have a sense of the fear, ask anxiety to go a little deeper with you. Ask anxiety, *And if this feared scenario happens, what will that* mean *about me as a person?* Listen. Breathe. Perhaps it means you are unsafe. Maybe it means you're unworthy. Maybe it's that you aren't in control. Listen without judgment. You are not trying to rationalize right now. You are listening to understand.

Once you have a clear picture of what your anxiety fears, thank your anxiety for showing up today and providing you with this important information. Ask your anxiety if it has anything else it wants to share with you right now.

When you are ready, open your eyes and return your attention to your surroundings.

With the experience fresh in your mind, take out your journal and answer the following reflection questions:

1. How accessible was your anxiety today? Did it feel louder or more distant than in past exercises? If it was more distant, what do you need to adjust the next time you approach this exercise to make it safer for your anxiety to communicate with you?

2. What information did you gather about what your anxiety fears?

3. Can you see how you and your anxiety share a common goal? (Avoiding rejection, feeling safe, and the like.) What is that common goal?

4. Was there anything that surprised you about this exercise?

Exploring Fundamental Fears

When exploring the fears of your anxiety, it's important to get to the most fundamental fear. The fundamental fear is exposed when we peel back the superficial layers of our fears and uncover a negative core belief about ourselves, others, or the world. The fundamental fear also helps make sense of the intensity and urgency our anxiety adopts. For example, if we revisit the example of my anxiety during professional meetings, my initial fear was of sounding stupid in my internship meetings. Once I went deeper, I found that if I sounded stupid, it meant that I would be laughed at, which meant that I would be rejected, which meant I am defective in some way. At the core, I didn't fear sounding stupid; I feared not being good enough. Sounding stupid was just a means to my biggest fear. A symptom of the fear rather than the fear itself. Once I understood this fundamental fear, the intensity of my anxiety started to make more sense. My anxiety was responding to the idea that I was not good enough, not just that I could be laughed at. Once I uncovered the fundamental fear, I could then explore other times I felt not good enough, which reinforced this fear. The point is, if we don't know what the fundamental fear is, we won't have an accurate picture of what our anxiety is actually responding to and working to protect us from.

You can uncover your fundamental fear by asking *If this happens, what does it say about me as a person?* To ensure that you get to the root, you may continue to ask your anxiety, *What happens then?* For example, if it is showing you a situation in which you put effort into your school work and then fail the class, ask it, *What happens if I fail the class?* Perhaps it answers, *You will disappoint everyone.* Then you might ask, *And if I disappoint everyone, what happens then?* It may then say, *You're a disappointment.* To take it a step further and really get to the root, you might ask, *And if I'm a disappointment, what does that say about me as a person?* The answer: *You're inadequate.* Failing the class, then, is not the root fear. Failing the class is how your anxiety is manifesting, just as a weed manifests above the ground where we can see it. Underneath the soil is the fear of being inadequate or defective—which is one of the four categories of *negative cognitions* defined by Francine Shapiro:

- Defectiveness; that is, the belief *I am inadequate, I am not good enough,* or *I am not lovable.*

- Responsibility; that is, the belief *I did something wrong* or *It's my fault.*

- Safety; that is, the belief *I can't trust anyone, I am in danger,* or *I am not safe.*

- Control/choice; that is, the belief *I am not in control* or *I am powerless.*

Fundamental fears take the form of these negative cognitions. And negative cognitions are always "I" statements. For example, *I'm not good enough* versus *He doesn't love me.* If you don't yet have an "I" statement, it likely means you need to continue to go deeper and explore what that *means* about you if that belief were true. You can use the questions *What does that say about me as a person?* and *What happens then?* interchangeably, based on which seems to fit better for your situation. Either one should help you uncover the negative cognition associated with your fear.

Let's say you experience heightened anxiety in your intimate relationship. You go inside and ask anxiety what it fears, and it responds,

He's going to leave you! You then ask, *And if he leaves me, what happens then?* Your anxiety responds, *You'll be all alone!* You ask, *And if I'm all alone, what does that say about me as a person?* Your anxiety may respond, *You're unlovable.*

In this case, the root fear that your anxiety is trying to protect you from is being unlovable. This manifests when your intimate partner has not responded to your text in several hours and your mind starts going to worst-case scenarios. You might feel compelled to run from the relationship, because if you get out first, you can't be broken up with and therefore you've dodged the feeling of being unlovable. Anxiety is often working to protect you from these kinds of bigger, scarier feelings. If you try to solve anxiety by challenging your thoughts about what may be happening when your partner is MIA, you are only working with what's above the surface, rather than the actual fear: of being unlovable.

To move on to the next phase of this work, where anxiety will show you where it is frozen in time, you must have accurate information about what is keeping it frozen in the first place. You have to understand the fundamental fear, not just the symptoms. This requires an open mind and a willingness to get uncomfortable. After all, you may be exposing your most vulnerable, painful fears from which you have been trying to escape for years. If, after learning more about these fundamental fears, you feel the need to revisit the Exploring Fear exercise earlier in this chapter, please do so.

On one hand, uncovering your fundamental fears is a stepping stone to reaching the ultimate goal: becoming unstuck from your past experiences and relieving yourself of the anxiety associated with them. On the other hand, understanding what is really driving your symptoms can be a huge point of awareness and healing in itself. For example, let's say you were having a text message conversation with your intimate partner. It's early in your relationship, and you shared a detail about your personal life that felt vulnerable. After you send this text, your partner stops responding, and the more time passes without a response, the greater your anxiety becomes. You may start wondering, *Was that too much?* Prior to engaging in the exercise in this chapter, you may have very little awareness about what is actually causing your anxiety; you just know that you feel very uncomfortable and might feel compelled to send your partner rapid-fire texts like "Sorry if that was too personal LOL." The more time passes without a response, the more you might feel inclined to make other desperate attempts to soothe your anxiety. Once you do this work and have more awareness of what is typically underneath your relationship anxiety, you may be able to go inside, explore what is actually happening, and remember that you fear being unlovable. Then you will more likely be able to engage in some mental dialogue that imparts logic and suggests that there are a thousand reasons why your partner may not be responding that do not indicate you are unlovable.

Anxiety has been trying to alert you to past little t traumas where these fundamental fears originated, and it is simultaneously working hard to protect you from feeling the emotions associated with them. Once you uncover these fundamental fears, it can feel nerve-racking to your anxiety, because now you are in touch with what it was working hard to prevent you from feeling. At this stage, anxiety will sometimes up the ante in its efforts to protect you. You might notice that your anxiety feels heightened as you move through these exercises. If it becomes overwhelming, you can always take a break and return to the self-soothing exercises in chapter 2. If it feels safe to continue, you can acknowledge that this is a normal part of the process, and that sometimes it feels worse before it gets better. You can be reassured that this work may feel threatening *and* that doing it does not actually pose any danger. After all, you are *revisiting* memories, not reexperiencing them. By uncovering these boulders keeping you stuck, you will help your anxiety become unstuck, and, as a result, it will not have to work so hard.

Where Does Your Fundamental Fear Come From?

Once you have uncovered the fundamental fear underneath your anxiety, you will then work to understand where this fundamental fear originated. The method I like to use in my therapy practice for uncovering past unresolved wounds was developed by Francine Shapiro; it is called the *float back technique* (Shapiro, 2012). The float back technique will allow you to uncover earlier little t traumatic experiences that are the boulders keeping you stuck and responding to past events as if they are current threats. These boulders are the experiences in your past from which you learned these negative beliefs about yourself. They are what anxiety is working so hard to protect you from. These experiences are existing in their own memory networks, unable to integrate with your adaptive memory networks, and causing your present symptoms. When you're doing this exercise, it's important to have a pen and paper nearby so that as anxiety shows you the boulders keeping it stuck, you can make a note of them and return to them individually to do the work that is required to become untethered.

Now that your anxiety has showed you its most fundamental fear, you need it to show you where this fear originated and became reinforced over time. You can think of this fundamental fear as being its own memory network, and you are going to ask anxiety to show you all of the memories that exist within that network—in other words, all of the times you felt defective or unlovable or unsafe. As you might imagine, this can be an uncomfortable exercise. Set yourself up for success here— bite off only as much as you think you can chew. You are not expected to come out of this exercise with a crystal-clear picture of every life event that has contributed to your anxiety over time. Take things slowly, and do not overexert yourself in this exercise. Perhaps anxiety will show you one boulder, and you will need time and space before you feel ready for it to show you another. It may be useful to return to some of the soothing exercises in chapter 2 when you need a break from this exercise. It's important to maintain trust between you and your anxiety, and if you push yourself too hard, it can cause a tear in the relationship, only reinforcing the perceived need to avoid this work in the future.

Come up with some ground rules for this exercise. Let your anxiety know that you are willing to allow it to lead you into some uncomfortable memories, and you trust it to show you what you need to see. If this exercise becomes too overwhelming, you will let it know that you need to back off and out for now and will revisit the exercise at a later time. Ask it to have patience with you as you approach this new, unfamiliar territory. Hold true to your word, backing out of the exercise if and when it becomes overwhelming. This is not a race. (You can also find an audio version of this exercise to download in the online free tools at http://www.newharbinger.com/48756.)

EXERCISE: Float Back

Find a place in your home or office that is free of distractions. In a comfortable seated position, close your eyes if you'd like, and notice your breath. Stay with your breath for as long as feels necessary. Then turn your attention inward and see if you can connect with your anxiety. As always, do not force it. If your anxiety is hiding today, just notice what it feels like to experience the absence of anxiety. Once you can connect with it, notice where and how it is showing up today. If you are having difficulty connecting to it, think of a recent experience in which you felt anxious. See if you can connect to that feeling again.

Once you have made the connection, take note of how you feel toward your anxiety. Can you be compassionate and curious toward it? Imagine sending these emotions toward it. Let it know that you're going to allow it to guide you into your past experiences to show you where it is stuck.

Share with your anxiety how you feel about engaging in this exercise, and let it know that you'd like to cover some ground rules. Tell your anxiety that this is very important work, and it's equally important to do this work carefully and with attention to your nervous system. Let it know that you're going to strive to remain time oriented in the present, bearing witness to these past experiences rather than becoming fused with your anxiety. If at any time you lose orientation to the present and you begin to relive these memories, that's an indicator to you that you might need to back out and reground yourself. Share with your anxiety how you will alert it to the need to back out, if it comes up.

Ask your anxiety if, for its part, there are any ground rules it wants to set with you. Listen. Breathe. Let your anxiety know that, once you begin, you're going to be writing down what it shows you, so that you can be sure you make note of the boulders accurately and thoroughly. When you are ready to do the untethering work, you will give each boulder the attention it deserves.

Now, ask anxiety to show you its fundamental fear. Maybe it has a few, but focus on the most pressing one for now—the one that seems to be driving your current symptoms of anxiety. Perhaps it's feeling unlovable, feeling not good enough, or feeling unsafe. Try to think of a recent experience that prompted that feeling, and embody that feeling now, even though it is uncomfortable.

Once you can tap into the emotions and body sensations associated with your fundamental fear, allow your mind to float back to an earlier time when you experienced a similar feeling. Turn your thinking brain off. You are not trying to think of an earlier memory; you are trying to *feel* for it. If your fundamental fear is of being unlovable, embody the feeling of unlovable and allow your mind and body to float back to an earlier time you felt unlovable. When a memory pops into your mind, open your eyes and write down the following:

1. Your age at the time of the experience (say, twenty-one)

2. A brief description of the experience (David ghosted me)

3. How upsetting this experience feels to you now on a scale from 0 through 10, if 0 is not at all or neutral and 10 is the most upsetting you can imagine (let's say your feeling rates a 6)

Close your eyes again and return to the exercise. Thank your anxiety for showing you this boulder, and let your anxiety know that you have it recorded and will return to it at a later time.

Next, bring back up the emotions and body sensations associated with this negative belief, and allow your mind to float back to an even earlier time you felt this way. Record the same three pieces of information about this earlier experience. Then close your eyes and float back even further. Write down each experience that comes to mind until you get to the very earliest time you can remember feeling your fundamental fear, which is usually in childhood. Keep in mind that you are reflecting on memories rather than experiencing this threat in the present. You are in a different time and space now, with the resources of an adult. You have more information and choices than you did when you were a child. You have the ability to keep yourself safe from danger, which was not true when you were a child. See if you can experience compassion for your younger self, who didn't know then what you know now.

You may complete this exercise in fifteen minutes, or it could take you multiple sittings. Once you cannot float back any further in time, you likely have a complete list of the boulders that have been keeping you stuck and are finished with this exercise.

Congratulations! This is a huge step in recovering from your anxiety.

Now use your journal to reflect on the following questions:

1. What was this exercise like for you?

2. Were there any surprises? Were there any memories that, until now, you hadn't remembered or realized were impacting you today?

3. How accessible were these memories to you? Did they come to you quickly and easily, or do you have a sense that you still do not have all of the information you need?

4. What is the earliest memory you have in which you felt this fundamental fear?

5.   Which of these memories feels most distressing to you? Was this
     surprising to you?

It is very common to have past wounds come to the surface that you would not have originally connected to your current anxiety. You might find yourself having thoughts like *What does that have to do with this?* or *I thought I was over that!* Resist the urge to use logic to discredit what your inner guide, anxiety, shows you. Remember, you are moving away from trying to solve anxiety with logic, and moving toward trusting your anxiety as an intuitive guide that will show you what it needs to heal.

Many of my clients have remarked at the end of therapy that creating this list of past painful experiences is the toughest part of the entire therapeutic process. From here on out, you will turn your attention and energy to only one boulder at a time. You will not move on from that boulder until it feels resolved enough to do so. For most clients, looking at one past painful experience in depth feels more manageable than the effort to take an inventory of all the times they felt unlovable or unsafe or defective. The point is, the exercise you just completed is no easy feat. If you were able to access the information, you should feel good about yourself, as you are one step closer to healing from your anxiety. If it doesn't feel complete yet, that is okay. Stay with the exercise until you feel confident that you have at least one boulder that you can work with. If more memories pop up later, you can add them to the list at that time.

A note on generational trauma and implicit memories: Research on generational trauma suggests that we can be psychologically impacted by trauma that happened to our caregivers in generations before us. If, while completing these exercises, you have a hard time pinpointing a single traumatic event in your past, and you have a sense that the trauma occurred before you existed, it could be an indicator of generational trauma. In this case, it might be helpful to imagine and write down the trauma your parent, grandparent, or ancestor endured that was passed down and its effects internalized by you.

Similarly, we can be impacted by trauma that happens in our first few years of life even if we don't have explicit or concrete memories of it. For example, if your mother had postpartum depression and was withdrawn and unresponsive to your needs during your first few weeks of life, you probably were psychologically impacted by this, but your memory of it will be implicit —more of a felt sense of unsafety than vivid, tangible memories of not being cared for.

If it feels appropriate to do so, you can include both generational and/or early implicit memories of childhood trauma on your trauma timeline—which you will create in the following exercise—even without being able to recall specific details of the memory.

EXERCISE: Create a Trauma Timeline as a Roadmap

When you are ready to move on from the float back exercise, organize your list of boulders into a *trauma timeline*. You can think of your trauma timeline as a visual depiction of the memory network that holds the painful emotions or experiences.

1.   Using the list you created in the last exercise, rearrange it in chronological order, starting with the earliest memory you can remember and ending with the most recent.

2.   Title this timeline with the fundamental fear (for example, "Unlovable Timeline").

3.   On this new timeline, record your age at the time of each event, a brief description of the event, and how upsetting the event feels to you now, using a 10-point scale.

If you have only a couple of boulders in this memory network, this may be a quick and easy exercise. If you have several, it may require several sheets of paper and a substantial amount of time. Remember: this is not a race. Once it's completed, you may have a trauma timeline that looks something like the one shown here.

"Unlovable" Timeline

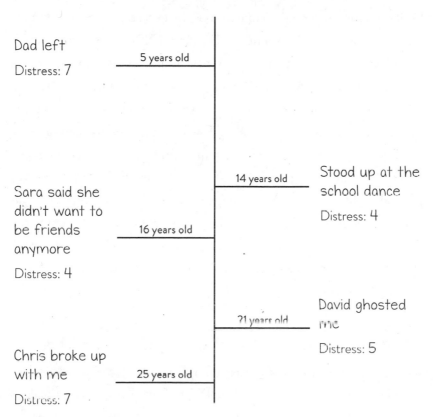

Dad left
Distress: 7

5 years old

14 years old

Stood up at the school dance
Distress: 4

Sara said she didn't want to be friends anymore
Distress: 4

16 years old

David ghosted me
Distress: 5

21 years old

Chris broke up with me
Distress: 7

25 years old

Creating your trauma timeline is important because it shows you first, the point from which your anxiety likely originated, and second, the events that have added to this memory network and perpetuated this negative belief over time. My client Sara was able to identify her earliest traumatic memory with blood at age eleven, and she had many other experiences with blood over the course of her lifetime that reinforced the fear and still caused her distress to think about. While we did not end up having to address each memory individually, it was important for her to know about them so that we could ensure, at the end of therapy, that they were no longer a source of distress for her that could continue to impact her current emotional state.

Knowledge is power when it comes to anxiety recovery, and the float back exercise provides a clear picture of the events that likely led to the symptoms we currently experience. Shapiro (2012) posits that, generally speaking, we have about ten to twenty unprocessed memories in our history that contribute to the majority of the suffering we experience in the present. You may have more or fewer depending on your age and history, but this gives you a sense of how long this exercise can take.

Equally as important as creating an accurate trauma timeline is creating a timeline of important events that are in the adaptive memory network—the experiences that shape what your logic knows to be true. These experiences often reinforce the opposite of your fundamental fear. For example, if you created a timeline of events stored in your "unlovable" memory network, you'll want to create a timeline of events in the "lovable" memory network.

EXERCISE: Creating an Adaptive Timeline as an Anchor

There are two good ways to assemble this timeline.

First, simply get out a piece of paper (or a journal page) and write down past events that created or reinforced the opposite feeling of your fundamental fear as they come to mind. For this timeline, record your age, a brief description of the event, and how lovable you felt on a scale of 0 through 10. If you have trouble accessing these memories, try closing your eyes, tapping into the sensation of feeling the *opposite* of your fundamental fear (feeling lovable, for example), and allowing your mind to float back to times in which you felt lovable, then recording them on paper.

For many people, creating the adaptive timeline can feel more challenging than creating the trauma timeline. If this is your experience, do not be discouraged. Do your best to find at least one adaptive memory, regardless of how fleeting or insignificant it seems. It can be something as small as a teacher who encouraged you or a childhood friend's parent who welcomed you to eat dinner with their family.

Once completed, your adaptive timeline may look something like the one shown here.

"Lovable" Timeline

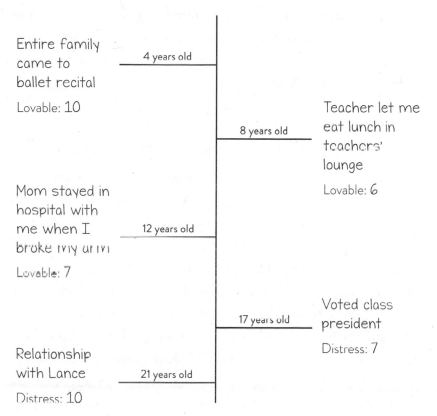

Entire family came to ballet recital

Lovable: 10

4 years old

8 years old

Teacher let me eat lunch in teachers' lounge

Lovable: 6

Mom stayed in hospital with me when I broke my arm

Lovable: 7

12 years old

17 years old

Voted class president

Distress: 7

Relationship with Lance

Distress: 10

21 years old

The second approach is to make a timeline of events that support what your logic knows to be true (*I am lovable*) and a separate timeline of events that have perpetuated what feels true when your anxiety is high (*I am unlovable*). This adaptive timeline of events can serve as an important anchor while you're doing this work and when you're experiencing anxiety in your day-to-day life. If you have a high-anxiety day in which you are feeling particularly unlovable, it may be useful to pull out your adaptive timeline and review the past experiences that have indicated otherwise. To take it a step further, you can close your eyes and embody the feelings that come to mind when you really put yourself back into these pleasant experiences, and allow that feeling to course throughout your body and expand.

Because anxiety can feel all-consuming when you experience it, it can be useful to remember times when you felt differently. This can be soothing because although you may be experiencing a lot of anxiety now, the adaptive timeline is a reminder that it has not always been this way and it will not always be so.

What If You Have Multiple Fundamental Fears?

Most people have more than one fundamental fear. For example, you may get relationship anxiety that boils down to a fundamental fear of being unlovable, and you may also experience some test anxiety that uncovers a fundamental fear of being not good enough. Although the sensations these fears produce might feel very similar, they are separate fundamental fears and likely exist in separate memory networks. If you uncover multiple fundamental fears, you will need to create two time-lines, one trauma and one adaptive, for each fear you identify. For example, you may create a Not Good Enough trauma timeline and a Good Enough adaptive timeline. You may also create an Unlovable Trauma Timeline and a Lovable Adaptive Timeline. You can revisit the Exploring Fear and Float Back exercises to uncover the fundamental fears and the associated past experiences stored in that memory network. You will work on one fundamental fear at a time as you enter the next phase of the work; in that phase, you will revisit these past boulders one by one and work to become unstuck from them.

Congratulations on making it this far; you are doing great. This is not easy work. If this does not come as easily or as quickly as you had hoped, be gentle with yourself. Diving into our past experiences may feel counterintuitive. And it takes time and patience—two things that our anxiety does not always have to spare. You may need to return to these exercises time and time again before feeling like you have documented a clear timeline of boulders to move forward with.

You will know you are ready to begin the untethering work in the following chapter when you:

- Can experience your anxiety as separate from you

- Can feel curiosity and compassion toward your anxiety

- Have identified a fundamental fear(s)

- Have an idea of where this fear originated and the experiences that have reinforced it over time

healing wounds together

Some would argue that once you have gotten to this point in the work, the hardest part is behind you. In creating a trauma timeline, you have gotten past the uncomfortable truth that your past experiences may hold the key to unlocking and releasing your anxiety. You likely have accepted that you probably do need to go back there. You have demonstrated willingness to dive into those past experiences, even though doing so brings up uncomfortable emotions and might feel counterproductive. All of this is something to be celebrated.

It is not uncommon for people to resist diving into their past experiences. I often work with clients who ask, "What can I do about my anxiety?" When I propose the idea of leaning into anxiety, getting to know it better, and exploring where it is stuck in the past, I sometimes get a perplexed look followed by a reiteration, "Okay, but what do I actually *do* about it?" Generally speaking, people do not want to look backward. It's not in our nature. We are conditioned to look ahead, to set goals and accomplish them. But you have tried that. You've attempted to outrun and extinguish your anxiety. You have told it that it doesn't make any sense. You've tried working harder, pushing through, doing more. And you have decided to open your mind to the possibility of approaching it another way. At this point in the work, if you've been doing the exercises you have likely already made leaps and bounds of progress, and for that I commend you.

Having created a timeline of events that have contributed to and reinforced your anxiety over time, you are ready to begin the untethering work. When you get to this stage, it is like having your own personal blueprint for healing from your anxiety.

If you haven't already, thank your anxiety for showing up and cooperating in showing you where it is stuck in trauma time. Because of your anxiety's willingness to communicate with you, you have an opportunity to do what you need to do to get you both unstuck. You can't do it without anxiety as your guide, and your anxiety definitely cannot work less hard without your willingness to explore where it came from. The next step in this work, the untethering, is mutually beneficial in that it will allow you to live a happier, healthier life with some freedom from anxiety, while allowing anxiety the freedom to kick back and relax a little rather than constantly alerting you to danger.

Note that the untethering work is almost always easier to navigate when you are working with a skilled therapist. Should you get stuck in this chapter or anywhere else while navigating this work, it may be an indicator that you could use a therapist's support. Keep in mind that we all have times when we aren't able to guide ourselves out of a particular painful experience and require the support of others, and this work is no exception. I often hear new clients say "I knew I needed help because my normal means of coping haven't been working for this particular issue."

You might find that you are able to make good progress in untethering from some of your boulders, but there are one or two that you cannot get unstuck on your own. Perhaps seeing a therapist for a couple of sessions could cause a shift that you need in order to return to this work on your own. It could also be that you experience a clinical mental health condition that this self-help work is not suited for, such as complex posttraumatic stress disorder (CPTSD), OCD, or a dissociative disorder. Regardless of what is preventing you from making progress in this work, a licensed therapist from whom you seek individual, personalized care will support you in reprocessing trauma memories in a way this book cannot.

That said, Francine Shapiro acknowledges in her self-help book *Getting Past Your Past* (2012) that the processing of past trauma memories "doesn't only have to take place in a therapist's office." She says, "Many things can happen in our everyday lives that cause our emotions to change and insights to occur." These can include new experiences that enter and reinforce your adaptive memory network, profound life experiences that shape you and cause you to view the world in a new way, or simply a series of small shifts in perception that come naturally with the passage of time.

Knowledge Is Power

Many people make progress in their emotional health simply by gaining an understanding of what is contributing to their pain, which you have done in the last chapter. For example, when you experience anxiety, it may be enough for you to be able to say to it *Ah, you again. I know why you're here. You're alerting me to that time in seventh grade when I was mocked after school. I can see how you think this situation might pose that same danger, but I've evaluated the risk, and I think we're in the clear.*

Perhaps you have already gained more insight into your anxiety and have experienced shifts that will be more than enough to change your relationship with it moving forward. I have had clients get to this stage in therapy, when they have a greater understanding of why their symptoms came to be and how they're impacting them today, and decide that they feel well equipped enough with this key information alone to discontinue the therapeutic process without ever doing the untethering work. Increased awareness, by itself, can be what allows you to move forward in your life with less anxiety and greater spontaneity and ease, as you so deserve. My hope is that you have already started to notice some minor shifts in how you experience and relate to anxiety that will prove useful in your life, regardless of how far you get in the following untethering work.

Most people, however, feel empowered by the increased awareness and education, but still need help addressing the source of anxiety so that they can eradicate the symptoms. I've heard countless times in my therapy practice "I know where this comes from and why it's happening. But I still can't stop it." In these cases, anxiety is no longer a puzzle to be solved. In fact, its origins may be crystal clear. If you sense that you have good insight into your anxiety but still need to go deeper into this work to fully heal it, this chapter will be helpful to you. I will guide you through the next step in the work and will offer an opportunity for you to revisit these past wounds safely so that you can become unstuck from them. In doing so, you will reassure your anxiety that it can live with you in the present, doing its job in alerting you to danger only when danger actually exists.

The untethering work in this chapter will include the following steps in this order:

1.   First, I will teach you how to access a calm, centered internal state which will prepare you to do the untethering work successfully. If you cannot access this state easily, we will come up with a representation of what this state would be like for you.

2.   You will connect with your anxiety and work to establish mutual compassion.

3.   You will then allow your anxiety to guide you into your stuck memories, one at a time. You will bear witness to the memories in which anxiety is stuck, then explore what you needed but didn't get at the time of the event. You will then uncover ways in which you can help meet those needs now.

4.   Finally, you will bring your anxiety with you into the present, where the danger is no longer happening.

Untethering

The first step in the untethering work is to get in touch with the most centered, calm version of yourself. Internal family systems (IFS) therapy calls this state *self-energy* and purports that everyone has it already within; it does not need to be created or cultivated. According to IFS, you know you are in self-energy when you experience eight Cs: curiosity, calmness, confidence, compassion, courage, creativity, connectedness, and clarity (Anderson, 2020). When you feel disconnected from self, it is because other parts of self (such as anxiety) are working hard inside and may be at the forefront, blocking you from experiencing the eight Cs. This can cause you to feel distant or detached from your calm and confident self-energy, but is not an indicator that self-energy does not exist. It's important to note that not everyone feels the eight Cs whole-heartedly even when in self-energy, and that is not a requirement for you either. The better question is, can you tap into curiosity, calmness, confidence, and the rest? You do not have to experience all of these all of the time.

It may be that this calm, centered version of yourself is just ordinary you minus anxiety. Perhaps you know self-energy very well because you experience this version of yourself often when your anxiety is well managed. If you experience anxiety related to a specific experience, such as public speaking, it may be that you are relatively cool, calm, and collected most of the time until it is time to talk in front of a group, in which case your anxiety hijacks your self-energy. Or perhaps you experience more generalized anxiety that feels constant, and the possibility of being centered and free of anxiety feels so foreign to you that it's causing you anxiety just to think about it! Regardless of how accessible self-energy feels to you now, there are different exercises that will help you get in touch with this version of you in a way that is necessary for untethering. I will guide you through these exercises now.

Now, let's come up with an image and felt sense of your highest-functioning, centered self. There are many ways to do this, and I've provided the following four exercises as options for this step in the work. I recommend that you read through all of them and then decide which feels like it will work best for you. You can certainly try all four of them and learn by doing which works best. The more resources you have, the better, so don't be afraid to spend too much time here. If none of these feels accessible, it may be that you need to revisit these exercises at a later time. Remember: this is not a race. (You can also find an audio version of these exercises to download in the online free tools at http://www.newharbinger.com/48756.)

EXERCISES: Find Your Most Centered Self

Option #1

Find a place in your home or office that is free of distractions. In a comfortable seated position, close your eyes, and turn your attention inward. Notice any thoughts, feelings, and body sensations you may be having. If you notice any unpleasant thoughts, just allow them to pass by as quickly as they came in. If you experience any anxiety or other uncomfortable emotions, simply acknowledge them and let them know that you are aware of their presence. Then ask these unpleasant emotions one by one if, for the purposes of this exercise, they would be willing to ease up and give you some space so that you can connect with your self-energy. Ask permission rather than demand this from them. You're not asking these emotions to go away, but rather to simply become unfused from you so that you can observe them from a place of curiosity.

Notice what it feels like for them to ease up for you. If these emotions aren't willing or able to give you space right now, perhaps it is not the right time or place for you to engage in this exercise. Once these uncomfortable emotions have stepped aside, turn your attention back to your breath, allowing it to continue to flow naturally.

Notice the experience of feeling calm, curious, and centered. This is self-energy. It is a deep inner knowing that has always been there and will always be there. Notice where it is showing up in your body. Perhaps it is located in your heart or solar plexus, or maybe it rests somewhere in your mind or elsewhere in your body. Or it could be a sensation that permeates your entire body. You might experience it as eternal, conscious, and intelligent. Maybe it is playful, sensitive, and creative. This part of you is calm and connected. Breathe into it, allowing it to expand. Just notice.

Now notice what image is associated with this part of you. Perhaps it looks like you in a certain time and space, or maybe it's an energy flowing through you like water. It could be a bright white light radiating from within or a solid, unwavering force like a mountain. Keep noticing this centered part of you.

Now turn your attention to how it feels to be connected to this part of you. Perhaps there is a warmth or a tingling sensation coursing throughout your body. Breathe. Notice any sounds associated with this part of you. Perhaps you notice a soft buzzing, or maybe there is stillness and silence. Spend a few more moments connecting with this part of you. Then take a mental snapshot of this version of you, which exists so freely, calmly, and confidently, so that you can return to this part of you at a later time.

Finally, thank this inner wisdom for showing up today, and let it know that you'll be connecting with it again very soon.

Many people find it hard to access the sensation of calm early in this work. If this first exercise was not accessible for you, I invite you to give this next one a try.

Option #2

As preparation, revisit one of the adaptive timelines that you created in chapter 5, particularly one that outlines experiences in which you felt safe, okay, and/or enough. Choose the event on the timeline that feels most powerful to you now.

> Find a place in your home or office that is free of distractions. In a comfortable seated position, turn your attention to your breath. Close your eyes and bring to mind that positive experience. Don't just think about this experience; try to feel into it again. Put yourself back there and notice how it felt to be lovable, worthy, enough. Really get a felt sense of it. Let the feelings you had at that time course through you now. You are just as lovable, worthy, and *enough* now as you were then.

> If your brain starts to make any negative associations, just notice them, like railroad cars on a passing train. Let them go, and turn your attention back to the pleasant feelings associated with this memory. Notice where you feel these sensations in your body. Perhaps they bring a warmth or a vibration. Maybe they feel like stillness.

> Create a snapshot of the version of you that felt these feelings. Perhaps it's an image of a younger you, or an image that represents the feelings this memory brings you now, like an anchor or a bright light. Notice as many details about this snapshot as you can, so that you can return here at a later time.

When working on option #2, it's important that the image you come up with does not become compromised by a negative association. This is the same concept we discussed in the Calm Place Visualization exercise in chapter 2. For example, if you begin thinking of a memory in which you felt completely lovable, and then your thoughts wander to how this was an exception and you are actually not truly lovable, try to bring your attention back to the feeling of being lovable. If this is not possible and the memory is now associated with a painful emotion instead, it may not be a useful resource for you in this work. If this happens, do not spend more time on it; simply move on to another pleasant memory on your adaptive timeline or to a different exercise altogether.

The next exercise is another version of the second option. Rather than revisiting an earlier version of yourself, however, this exercise invites you to tap into your future older, wiser self.

Option #3

Get comfortable, close your eyes, and turn your attention inward. Notice any thoughts, feelings, and sensations you may be having. If you notice any unpleasant thoughts, just acknowledge them and allow them to pass by. If you experience any anxiety or other uncomfortable emotions, simply acknowledge them and let them know that you are aware of their presence. Then imagine asking them, one by one, to give you a little space for the purposes of this exercise.

Next, create an image in your mind of an older, wiser version of yourself. It could be you five years from now or fifty years from now. Imagine this older version of you as having been through many important experiences that have allowed that self to develop great knowledge and wisdom. Imagine your older self as being mostly freed from anxiety and fear, and being content with yourself and the world around you. Find awe in the inner beauty, awareness, and insight that this self possesses. Breathe.

Now imagine this older, wiser version of you coming into the present moment with you. Perhaps you sit in adjacent chairs while sipping cups of tea together. Maybe you hold hands or hug. Imagine this older version of you telling you what you need to hear right now. Notice how it feels to have that self close. Breathe. Allow these pleasant emotions to course through you, and allow yourself to be comforted and soothed by this supportive resource that is your older, wiser self. Take as much time as you need here.

Now create a mental snapshot of yourself experiencing the pleasant emotions you feel when you are with this resource. Try to encapsulate the images and associated feelings and body sensations in this snapshot. Keep it close so that you can return here when you are ready to continue the work.

If these three exercise options were not accessible for you today, it could be that now is not the right time and space for the untethering work, and it may be more appropriate to return to it at a later time. It could also mean that your anxiety and perhaps other emotions have been working so hard and for so long that it's tough to imagine yourself without them, even in a different time and space. When this is the case, it can be useful to find external resources that can help you tap into the sensations of calm rather than relying on inner resources. If this feels true for you, I'll invite you to try the following alternate technique for getting in touch with your most centered self.

Option #4 (Alternate)

Get comfortable, close your eyes, and turn your attention inward. Notice any thoughts, feelings, or sensations you may be having. Act as a mindful observer of your inner experience rather than clinging to or pushing away anything. Breathe.

Now bring to mind the image of someone or something you have had or imagine having in your life that offers unconditional protection and love. It could be something imaginary, like your favorite Disney character or superhero. It could be someone special in your life who provided this love, care, and protection to you in the past—like a teacher or a childhood friend's parent—or in the present, like a current intimate partner or friend. This resource could be someone who is no longer alive, like a deceased family member or pet. It could be a higher power, like God or a spirit guide. It matters less who or what this resource is and more the felt sense that you have when you imagine them being with you. Perhaps this resource comes to you immediately, or maybe you need more time. Take as much time as you need. The goal is to experience an increased sense of safety and calmness when they are with you.

Once you have this resource in mind, imagine them coming into the present with you now. Bring them nearby and notice the sensations you experience when they are close. Breathe. Allow the pleasant emotions to course through you, and allow yourself to be comforted and soothed by this supportive resource. Perhaps you want to interact with them in some way, or maybe it is enough to simply feel their presence.

Create a mental snapshot of yourself experiencing the pleasant emotions you feel when you are with this resource. Try to encapsulate the images and associated feelings and body sensations in this snapshot. Keep it close so that you can return here when you continue the work.

Ideally, your own "self-energy" will become the resource that you need in order to help your anxiety heal from the wounds it is stuck in. This is the goal because if and when you are done with this work, and you're in a situation where you encounter anxiety that does not fit the facts of the situation, it is usually most simple to tap into your centered self to help manage it. Your centered self will always be with you, to assist you in working through whatever challenges you are facing at any given time. This makes it an invaluable resource.

If, for example, you use your spouse as an external resource for the untethering work you are doing now, and a year from now you are going through a hard time with your spouse and are having anxiety as a result, it is likely that your spouse will not be the best resource to help you revisit this work when needed. However, when it's not yet possible to access your own centered self, option #4 can be a useful tool to identify a strong resource that can help you become untethered from the boulders that are your past traumatic experiences. Identifying an external resource will not require you to be able to tap into self-energy if that feels inaccessible. However, as much as you can, it's important to turn your attention to the way you feel in the presence of this resource, rather than the resource itself. This way, the resource shifts from an outside person to an inside feeling and can be more universally applicable.

After completing one or more of these exercises, take out your journal and reflect on the following questions.

1.   What was it like to experience self-energy? How did you know when you were tapped in to your most centered self?

2. What emotions did you experience when you were connected to your self-energy?

3. What body sensations are associated with your centered self?

4. Write about or draw a picture of the mental image you came up with.

5. How do you think this state of being might help you untether yourself from past boulders keeping you stuck?

Now that you have an image and felt sense of your most centered self, it's time to connect this version of you to the part of you that is anxious. To do this, I will guide you through an exercise adapted from the dissociative table technique created by George Fraser. The technique is designed to provide a forum for various parts of self to communicate and work together in healing trauma (Martin, 2012). Both your most centered self and your anxious self will revisit these wounds together. You can think of it as two forces with a common goal, teaming up to do what needs to be done to achieve that goal. This untethering takes teamwork and communication, which you will facilitate in the following exercise. (You can also find an audio version of this exercise to download in the online free tools at http://www.newharbinger.com/48756.)

EXERCISE: Introducing Your Most Centered Self to Anxiety

Find a place in your home or office that is free of distractions. In a comfortable seated position, turn your attention to your breath. Close your eyes and feel yourself melting into the surface you're resting on. Notice how the furniture or floor beneath you is holding you up, supporting you. Breathe.

Now imagine a meeting place where you will bring together your anxiety and your most centered self or resource. It is a space with exactly enough seats or room for you. Make sure this meeting place feels comforting and calm. Maybe it is a boardroom; maybe it's a treehouse. Once you have a meeting place in mind, ask the anxious part of you, who will be in charge of leading you back to the boulder you are tethered to, to enter the meeting place with you and take a seat wherever it would like. When it does, thank your anxiety for showing up today.

Next, bring your most centered self or external resource to the meeting place. This part will take the role of assisting anxiety in the untethering. Allow these two parts of you to come together and see if they can experience mutual compassion for one another. Acknowledge the common goal of becoming untethered from these boulders. Maybe it's a goal of feeling lovable, or good enough, or safe. Acknowledge the goal of this work: anxiety will not have to work quite as hard, and you will experience some relief. Ask your anxiety to notice the resource you brought in, and the fact that it has a new team member—one that it didn't have in the past—to support it now. Ensure that these two parts have a supportive relationship before you proceed. If there is any contention, they will need to spend more time together, with you as the mediator, until they have resolved any issues so they can move forward as a team. Once they can experience mutual curiosity and compassion, it is safe to continue.

Now that you have introduced your most centered self to your anxiety, take out your journal and reflect on the following questions.

1. How accessible was your anxiety today? Your centered self?

2. What was it like for you to create a meeting place for the parts of yourself?

3. What was the felt sense of the relationship between these parts of self?

4. Did you feel blocked from this exercise at any point? If so, what can you do to move forward (for example, try again later, eliminate distractions, explore the part of me that's fearful)?

5. Do you have a sense that these two parts share a common goal?

6. Do you have a sense that these two parts are capable of working together on a team, or is more relationship building needed?

The introduction of your most centered self to your anxiety can feel complicated. When we go inside, it is common for multiple different emotions to come up, even conflicting ones. Perhaps there was a part of you that felt angry. Or maybe there's a part of you that feels indifferent and isn't sure that it wants to go further in this work. Or perhaps the blocked sensation we discussed in chapter 5 is happening because this work feels threatening. As we discussed in earlier chapters, you shouldn't expect this work to feel seamless; in fact, it is often messy. However, it should feel accessible. To make this determination, you might go inside and ask yourself, *Is there any part inside that does not want us to revisit these boulders?* If any part of you screams in opposition, it is a good indicator that this part of you needs to feel a little more safe before moving forward. If you get an agreement, even a begrudging one, it is safe to move forward.

If you have a part of self that you sense is interfering in some way, you will need to spend some time with that part before you go charging ahead in the work. You'll want to explore what the part's job is, what it is fearful of, and what it needs from you in order to feel okay with continuing. Come up with an agreement with the part about how you will proceed in a way that is safe for all. Once you sense that all parts of self are on board to revisit your past boulders, it is time to continue the work.

How Can You Know Where to Start?

Your most centered self and your anxiety have to come up with a game plan for which boulders should be addressed first. The good news is that you have already written down a map of your boulders: your trauma timeline. I will share with you a couple of theories on the order in which to best approach these boulders, so you can make an informed decision on where to start. There is no right or wrong answer here, so don't let making this decision hold you up.

The first theory suggests that if you tackle the earliest chronological memory on your timeline first, healing from that memory may have a cascading effect on later memories. In other words, if you connect the earliest trauma memory to an adaptive memory network, it may by default connect other, later trauma memories to that same adaptive network. This would mean that you could revisit one trauma memory, become untethered from it, and then realize that a subsequent memory spontaneously no longer causes you any distress, because it had been grouped in your brain with the original memory.

Another theory holds that you will get the most relief the fastest if you start with the memory on your timeline that causes you the most distress or anxiety now. It's likely that the "worst" memory on your timeline is currently the biggest contributor to your anxiety. Therefore, revisiting that memory first may offer the greatest and fastest relief. Francine Shapiro, in describing a roadmap for addressing past trauma in EMDR therapy, refers to these two potential starting places as "first or worst."

I recently worked with a client who had anxiety every time she felt sick or dizzy. On her trauma timeline was an incident three years earlier in which she had passed out in her bathroom after experiencing a bout of dizziness. She reported that since that incident, any slight indication that she could pass out again—dizziness, nausea, or lightheadedness—caused her anxiety to spike. The incident in which she passed out in her bathroom was listed on her trauma timeline as a distress level of 10 out of 10. Since this event three years before, she had experienced other related incidents that were less distressing, such as the time she got sick with the flu. Together we decided to first address the time she got the flu, as she wanted to have some practice with the untethering process prior to revisiting one of the scariest things that has happened to her. Once we completed the untethering of this memory, she felt confident to move on to the scarier ones.

When considering which boulder to address first, it's important to start with one that feels manageable. If there is a memory on your timeline that causes a distress level of 10 out of 10, and you feel a strong impulse to avoid it, honor that for now. Similarly, if you have a memory on your timeline that causes some detachment or emotional flooding when you think about it (a sign that you have exited your window of tolerance), that is probably not the best place to start either. In fact, that may be a memory that warrants the support of a professional therapist to reprocess. Conversely, if all of the memories on your trauma timeline cause a relatively low amount of distress, it may be that you can start with the one that causes the most distress, because it is likely still a manageable amount of distress that feels tolerable to revisit.

Take a look at your trauma timeline and the boulders listed, as well as their corresponding distress levels. Is there a boulder with a distress level of 4 to 6 that may be a good starting place? Make sure that both your most centered self and the part of you that is anxious agree on the starting place. You can do this by going inside and connecting with your most centered self or external resource and the anxious part of you. Let them know which memory you'd like to start with, and see if there are any objections. If there are, see if there are any ideas about where is a better starting place. Once you have a mutually agreed upon starting place, you can begin the next exercise. (You can also find an audio version of this exercise to download in the online free tools at http://www.newharbinger.com/48756.)

EXERCISE: Healing Wounds

Find a place in your home or office that is free of distractions. In a comfortable seated position, turn your attention to your breath. Close your eyes and feel yourself melting into the surface you're resting on. Notice how the furniture or floor beneath you is holding you up, supporting you. Breathe.

Now bring up the image of your meeting place. This place is calm and comfortable, with exactly enough space for all. First, imagine yourself in this meeting place. When you feel ready, imagine inviting your anxiety into the same meeting place. Imagine your most centered self or external resource in the meeting place with you. Ensure that you have permission to move forward by asking all parts if it's okay to proceed. If any part inside you objects to moving forward, explore what this part of you might need to feel it's safe to continue. Maybe it doesn't want to participate but is willing to watch from an adjacent room. Perhaps it wants to be able to speak up when it is time to back out. Maybe it needs to be with an external resource to provide protection as you revisit past wounds together. Do not force things; rather, ensure that you have permission from all parts of self to move forward.

Next, in your mind's eye, imagine anxiety leading you and this resource back to the boulder. Perhaps anxiety is in the front, with you and the resource following behind. Or maybe you are the leader, with anxiety giving you directions from behind. Maybe your most centered self or resource is leading, perhaps holding anxiety's hand or carrying it on its back, ensuring that it is safe. Maybe you ride in on a plane or a magic carpet. Go with whatever your imagination conjures up.

Let your mind float back to this earlier traumatic experience. Maintain the awareness that you are in a different time and space now than you were when this memory happened. You are revisiting the memory rather than reliving it.

When you get to the boulder, allow your anxiety to show you what it needs to. Be a supportive observer, a silent witness. Give your anxiety as much time as it needs to show you what is important about this experience. Breathe. If you notice any emotions coming to the surface, make space for them. Allow them to flow over you like ocean waves. If this becomes too overwhelming, try putting a partition between you and the memory. Perhaps you revisit the memory from behind a brick wall with one brick missing, allowing you to see through. Maybe you get on your magic carpet and hover above the memory, looking down on it.

Let your anxiety know that you and your resource are watching and listening and are here to bear witness to this experience. Take as much time here as you need to ensure that your anxiety has shown you everything it needs and wants to. Let anxiety know that it didn't have you at the time of the memory, but you are with it now. Listen. Stay present with it.

Now, ask your anxiety what it needed at the time of this experience but didn't get. Don't try to figure out the answer; instead, listen for it. Breathe. Maybe it needed a supportive adult to tell it everything was going to be okay.

Maybe it needed someone to keep it safe. Maybe it needed a hug. Allow anxiety to tell you what it needed. Breathe. Listen.

Now imagine providing to your anxiety what it needed then but didn't get. Take your time here. Breathe. Tell the younger you what they needed to hear. If needed, allow your external resource to step in and help. If this is a scary memory, allow the resource to provide protection. If it's a sad memory, allow the resource to console you. Use your wildest imagination as you revisit this boulder, letting happen whatever feels like it needs to happen. Let any emotions well up and flow over and out of you. Tell your anxiety that at the time of this memory, it was all alone, but now it has you, its biggest resource. Let it know that you're here with it and it won't ever have to be alone again. Breathe.

Spend as much time here as necessary. Do not rush this process. Anxiety might have a lot to show you, and it may need a lot from you now. Stay with this exercise until you feel some relief and closure. If it becomes too overwhelming, simply honor that and back out for now.

Then, when you're ready, ask your anxiety if it would like to be able to leave this memory in the past. If it says no, see what needs further addressing. Ask what else it needs to show you now. If it says yes, imagine doing anything more that feels necessary while in this memory.

Now imagine bringing anxiety out of this memory and into the present with you, where this danger no longer exists. Where does anxiety want to go? Perhaps it wants to go with you to a comforting place. You may return to your safe meeting place or somewhere different. Check in with your anxiety and see how it is feeling. Tell it that it won't ever have to go back there again.

Check in with the other parts of yourself, see if any of them were able to witness what just occurred, and survey their thoughts and feelings. Thank your anxiety for leading you back to this boulder, and thank your higher self and/or external resource for showing up and providing for your younger self what it has always needed. Rest now.

Now take out your journal and reflect on the following questions.

1. What was that experience like for you?

2. What did anxiety need to show you? What did it need from you now that it never got then?

3. Were you able to give anxiety what it needed? If so, how?

4. Was there any part of this exercise that felt inaccessible or blocked? If so, what is your sense of that?

5. What is important to you to remember from this exercise?

When It Doesn't Go as Planned

Don't be discouraged if you didn't get the results you were hoping for from this exercise. Sometimes it can take a few days for this new information and experience to fully integrate and for you to start to feel better. Many clients, immediately after completing this phase of the work, say they feel generally lighter and sometimes a little confused or disoriented. Then when I see them a week later, it is not uncommon for them to experience greater clarity and for this memory to feel much less distressing. It can take some time for your brain to integrate new information and connect old memories to adaptive memory networks.

Other times, there can be factors that get in the way of successful untethering. The first factor is when the memory you are revisiting becomes too overwhelming. This can cause you to exit your window of tolerance and enter hyperarousal (emotional flooding; fight or flight) or hypoarousal (emotional shutdown; freeze). When you exit your optimal healing zone and enter hyper- or hypoarousal, you are no longer reprocessing past trauma but are instead reliving it. This signals to your body that danger is imminent, causing your body to enter survival mode and elicit the fight, flight, or freeze response. When you are in survival mode, you cannot do this work safely or effectively.

If you think you exited your window of tolerance while working through this exercise, it is an indication that you need increased safety before proceeding. The exercises in chapter 2 will help activate your parasympathetic nervous system and bring you back to a more regulated, restful state. Remember that your window of tolerance can look different from day to day. If you are hungry, angry, lonely, or tired, or if you have more stressors than usual in your life, you may experience greater emotional vulnerability. This can reduce your capacity to revisit past trauma memories safely. It is important that you get the timing right. It may be that on one day this exercise is way too overwhelming, but the next day, after a full night's sleep, the work feels totally accessible. Listen to your body and make sure it's a good time to do this work.

If you have ensured that you are well rested and well fed and have your stressors relatively well managed but you are still finding this work to be too overwhelming, you can try a couple of strategies, called *emotional distancing* techniques. These are useful for keeping your nervous system more regulated, enabling you to do this work. These skills are designed to create some distance between you and the emotions associated with past traumatic events so that you can approach them safely. I briefly mentioned these emotional distancing techniques in the previous exercises; now let's delve into the details.

The first technique is to imagine some kind of barrier between you and the trauma memory. In the preceding exercise, I gave the example of imagining a brick wall between you and the memory, with you bearing witness to the memory through a hole in the wall the size of one brick. Many people report that imagining a barrier like this can help the memory feel more accessible, while remaining safe enough that the brain does not trigger a survival response. As you reexperience the memory with your highest self and/or external resource, it may become increasingly safe to imagine more bricks coming out of the wall. Perhaps eventually the wall will disintegrate completely, giving you full access to the memory. Other possible barriers between you and the memory can be a glass wall or a wall with a window in it for you to see through, or a canyon or a body of water.

Another emotional distancing technique is to imagine displaying the memory on a small TV or smartphone screen. Then you can watch the memory happen on the screen rather than experiencing it yourself through all your senses. The key here is that you have the power to change the channel or turn off the phone anytime the memory becomes too activating. You can imagine watching the trauma memory on the screen, while your higher self or external resource is with your younger self in the memory. Then, when it feels safe enough, you might imagine actually entering the memory yourself.

The final emotional distancing technique involves imagining the memory in black and white or otherwise muted in some way. Sometimes the colors of the experience can make it feel too vivid and can be overwhelming to your senses. Imagining the experience in black and white can tone down the associated emotions. A client I worked with reported that imagining the memory in black and white helped her remember that the memory is in the past, keeping her oriented to the present.

Another factor that can get in the way of successful untethering can arise when you have another part of you that is in a protective role and doesn't want you to access this memory. Rather than the memory feeling too vivid, this intervening part usually causes the memory to feel blocked. When this happens, it is important to turn your attention to the part of you that feels threatened by approaching this work and trying to gather more information about it. This would ideally happen in the meeting place prior to revisiting the memory. You might ask yourself *Are there any parts inside me that feel resistant to approaching this boulder?* If there is a part of you that screams *Yes!*, you will need to spend some time with that part and make sure you have its permission before proceeding. Otherwise, you can expect that it will do its best to keep you from accessing it. While this might be frustrating, it's important to remember that these parts of you are doing their very best to keep you safe. They just don't understand that revisiting a memory is actually not dangerous, just as a small child might not understand that their caregiver's leaving the room for a few minutes is not dangerous. Spending some time with this part and getting to understand its fears and what it needs from you in order to proceed safely will save you time (and emotional labor) down the line.

Perhaps this part would agree to proceed on the basis that you use one of the emotional distancing techniques just described. While doing this work, watch for some indicators that you may have a part like this: feeling sleepy, zoned out, or generally detached or disconnected from the process, or feeling panic or the need to run away.

If you are feeling like this exercise was helpful but the memory doesn't quite feel fully resolved, you may need to revisit the exercise and do something different. Peter Levine developed a therapeutic modality for releasing trauma responses that he named Somatic Experiencing, in which he posits that trauma gets stored in our bodies due to thwarted survival energy that is locked up in the body and needs to be released (Levine, 2020). Levine studied the stress response in the nervous systems of animals, who are under constant threat but do not develop PTSD. He came to understand that after animals enter the "freeze" survival response, if they survive the threat, they tremble and shake to discharge the energy that prepared them to fight or flee. He theorizes that in humans, when that energy is not released, it stays stored in the body, causing us to think we are still under threat. Somatic Experiencing is a comprehensive therapeutic modality that is performed by a trained professional; however, the concepts may resonate with you and provide some insight into what can be done to facilitate the releasing of trauma memories that feel stuck.

Many times when a client is revisiting trauma memories, they will get cues from their body about movements or actions they need to take, even if they can't logically understand why. In my own personal experience with releasing a trauma memory in therapy, I told my therapist I felt compelled to enter the fetal position. I have to admit, it was sort of awkward to say that and even more so to get into that position on the floor of his office. However, I had a sense that my body needed to get into that position to complete the movement it had needed to do at the time of the memory but didn't because it froze instead. Once I allowed myself to get into that position, the reprocessing happened.

Similarly, I once had a client who, while engaging in this work, felt the strong urge to scream at her mother. I could almost feel the pent-up energy in her body and could see that she needed to complete this movement. She too wanted to scream, but her adult self was holding back because she did not want to disturb the sessions in adjacent therapy offices. Because I could see this was an important part of this work for her, we went outside, and I invited her to scream there. I screamed with her. She did it several times, and I could see the emotional energy being released from her body each time.

As you approach this work, you too may feel compelled to complete the movement somehow. Maybe you feel like you physically want to shake it off; perhaps you need to scream, or cradle yourself, or punch a pillow. Other practices that can be useful for releasing energy stored in the body include exercise or movement, massage, reiki, and yoga. It's important to listen to your body and trust that it knows what it needs to do, and then create a space where it is free to discharge this energy in whatever way feels best. Our bodies are powerful and hold important information about our emotions and what is required to heal. Often our "doing" minds take over and neglect what our bodies are asking of us, simply because what they are asking doesn't make logical sense. As you navigate this work, I invite you to continually push your logical mind to the side and tap into the inner wisdom of your body's felt sense. It has the answers you seek.

Remember, this work is messy. You are probably feeling a mixture of emotions at this point—maybe lighter in some ways, perhaps more confused or perplexed, maybe relieved, maybe angry. One emotion that is very common to experience in this stage of healing is grief. Even if the processing you've done feels productive and helpful, the relief can be accompanied by grief about how the trauma has impacted you up to this point. I recall that at this stage in my own process, I had to grieve over how harsh I was to myself for years while sitting in professional meetings.

Grief about what anxiety has taken from you is necessary and adaptive, and it deserves to be acknowledged, just as any other emotion does. See if you can make space for whatever emotions you are feeling right now. If it feels helpful, take out your journal and try free-writing all of the thoughts and emotions you are experiencing; this can help you gain some clarity.

The work you have done thus far deserves to be celebrated. Diving into past experiences takes tremendous effort and courage, and it may seem easier to just keep on avoiding your anxiety. You have chosen the harder but necessary path, and that is something to be proud of.

Spend as much time as you need to on the untethering work in this chapter. Depending on your history of trauma, you may feel ready to move on from untethering now, or you may need to go through the steps outlined in this chapter with several more trauma memories. Feel free to take breaks! You are not a constant self-improvement project, and you deserve time and space for rest and leisure in addition to the healing work you are doing. If you need to take a break from revisiting past trauma before returning to another boulder, that is perfectly okay. It may be that the work you have done thus far has gifted you a new lens through which to see the world, and you might want to give yourself a few days or weeks to adjust to it before you move on to another memory.

When you're ready, take a look back at your trauma timeline and rerate the distress level associated with each memory. From that vantage point you can decide which memory, if any, to tackle next. Repeat the steps in this chapter until you feel little to no distress associated with each memory on your timeline. In general, if a past trauma memory causes a distress level of no more than 1 or 2, it may be okay to move on from it. Some memories will always hold some level of distress, because the fact that they happened is inherently sad or upsetting. They don't have to reach a distress level of 0 to be fully processed.

Once you feel satisfied with the distress level associated with the memories on your trauma timeline, it is time to start the future-oriented work. The following chapter will help you develop a working relationship with your anxiety moving forward so you can continue to reap the benefits of the processing work you have done thus far, and your anxiety will remain well managed enough to allow you the space and freedom to live your life to the fullest.

CHAPTER 7

a working relationship
with your anxiety

It is likely that revisiting past little t traumas brought up some big emotions for you. In fact, you may have experienced emotions that have been trapped inside for years. Perhaps your emotions felt rather straightforward, or maybe they were surprising, confusing, or conflicting. The path to healing from past trauma is not always predictable or linear, and neither are the emotions experienced along the way. Whether you tapped into deep sadness, fiery rage or fear, you can trust that the emotions you experienced were necessary. Though these painful emotions may not feel like progress in your healing, rest assured they come naturally with the work of learning and growing.

What Does Healing Actually Look Like?

After working through the exercises in chapter 6, your relationship to your trauma memories should have shifted in some way. Doing this work does not mean that you should forget the trauma or the way it impacted you, nor does it mean that you should feel grateful that it happened or experience any other pleasant emotions when you think about it. You may always wish it hadn't happened, and that is okay. It is more realistic that the outcome of healing from a trauma memory means it becomes less vivid and distressing. You may start to think about it in a new way.

It may become something that happened to you rather than something that defines you. You will realize that you are bigger than that past incident or situation.

One of my former clients used a tree metaphor to describe what healing felt like to her. She said that when she initially came to therapy, it felt like her life was a tree and her trauma was the main trunk. Every branch of her life was connected to and impacted by her trauma: her social relationships, work, and family. (Note that this was a big T trauma rather than a little t, and likely would have been beyond the scope of self-help work.) At the end of therapy she said her trauma became a smaller branch at the top of the tree. While it still had its place in her memory, it became an isolated experience that no longer touched every part of her life. She was now the trunk, and the branches were her experiences. Although this was a big T trauma, you should experience a similar shift in that your little t trauma no longer impacts you the way it did before.

Once there is a shift in the way you relate to your trauma, there is a good chance that the way you experience emotions will shift too. When a trauma memory integrates, it becomes stored in its correct time and place: the past. This means that your anxiety will stop responding to this traumatic memory as if it presents current danger. It will be able to assess current threats more accurately.

For example, let's say you revisited a past memory of being left out of a social group. Before this memory was resolved, you may have experienced anxiety when an ambiguous social situation triggered this past experience—say, not yet receiving an invitation to a friend's upcoming event. Once you have revisited and healed the wound of being left out when you were younger, you probably won't experience the same degree of anxiety when you are waiting to receive an invitation. You might have more adaptive thoughts, like *There is still a lot of time before the event. I may still receive an invitation. Or If I'm not invited, it won't be the end of the world. I don't really like gatherings anyway.*

Healing from past little t trauma memories does not mean you will experience a complete eradication of anxiety. To be human is to experience a wide range of emotions, anxiety included. It is inevitable and necessary. But once anxiety is no longer stuck in trauma time, it becomes useful. It will remind you of what is important to you and will prompt you to act in a way that is in line with your values. It will also alert you to danger that actually does exist, which, again, is an important survival mechanism.

You don't want anxiety to go away completely. To determine whether your anxiety warrants your attention and intervention, you can ask yourself the simple question *Does my anxiety fit the facts of the situation I am in?* For example, if you are anxious about whether you will get fired from your job after sleeping through a scheduled shift, that anxiety fits the facts, because your job is important to you and you need to pay your bills. You can problem solve it by reaching out to your boss, apologizing, and reiterating the job's importance to you. If you are anxious because your partner said he would be home in thirty minutes, but two hours have gone by without his arriving home, the anxiety fits the facts of the situation and would prompt you to make calls to make sure he is okay. Experiencing anxiety usually feels very uncomfortable, but that does not mean it is wrong and should be eliminated from your life.

This chapter will help you build a working relationship with your anxiety so that you can reap its benefits moving forward. Through this relationship, you will experience anxiety as no longer something to be feared or extinguished. While it may always be an uncomfortable experience, anxiety will become a key messenger in your life—a helpful signal that you learn to respect, honor, and trust.

Step One: Establishing a Communication Plan

The first step in building a working relationship with your anxiety is to establish a communication plan for future interactions with it. Having great communication with your anxiety is as important as having great communication with any other person in your life. It will help you avoid feeling like your anxiety is in control of your life and will help anxiety know that you care about it and realize the importance of what it has to say. When anxiety can trust that you will hear and understand it, and you can trust that anxiety will loosen its grip so that you can enjoy your life, living with anxiety becomes not so bad after all.

The nice thing about anxiety is that it usually follows predictable steps when it is trying to communicate with you. It's common for anxiety to come on gradually, as if it is trying to subtly nudge you to see something. Because it is not always logical, you may not automatically be able to put the pieces together and understand what it is trying to say. This is something that you will learn to do with practice.

Regardless of how quickly it escalates, anxiety always begins with a nudge. You might be objecting: *No way! What about panic attacks? They spring on me full-blown!* It can definitely feel this way. However, when I work with my clients to break down what led up to their panic attack, there is some subtle evidence that anxiety was building over a short time before the explosion happened. For example, a client I worked with recently told me that she drove to a birthday party to pick up her son. While waiting in the car for him to come outside, she started to feel panic coming on. She originally reported that it came out of nowhere; there were no apparent triggers. Because this anxiety did not fit the facts, we decided to do a little more digging. After examining the panic attack further, she said that she and her husband had gotten into an argument a few hours before, and the encounter was still weighing on her. Immediately following the argument, she had started having doubts about whether she was a good spouse and whether her marriage would last. She began to wonder if she wasn't a burden to everyone in her life. At this point, her anxiety sent the nudge—it pointed her to the threat of losing everyone she cared for. As would be the case for most of us, she didn't have awareness of what was happening in the moment, so she ignored her anxiety's nudges and later got into the car to start driving (another situation that caused her anxiety). As she continued to push her anxiety away, it became louder and louder until it evolved into panic.

Your anxiety probably manifests in your body in similar ways each time. Maybe it feels like butterflies in your stomach, a weight on your chest, a lump in your throat, a shaky voice, or jitters throughout your entire body. These body sensations may be the first sign that your anxiety is trying to communicate with you. No matter when, where, or how your anxiety manifests, having an intimate understanding of it will make you more responsive to it and ultimately contribute to a proactive, effective working relationship.

When you don't acknowledge or understand your anxiety's nudges, it will usually keep trying to get your attention. If you either fail to recognize or actively ignore these attempts, it will almost always just keep getting louder until you have to acknowledge it. At that point, it can feel like you have lost control and anxiety has taken over the driver's seat of your life. In some instances it may feel like anxiety goes from 0 to 100 within minutes. Other times it will become louder over a period of months or even years.

The goal in communicating effectively with anxiety is to be tuned in to it enough that you can acknowledge its subtle nudges. If you can make anxiety feel seen when it is small, it has no reason to make itself bigger to get your attention.

There may be periods in your life in which anxiety is relatively quiet and in the background. When this happens, you can trust that its needs are generally being met, and you may not need to be having ongoing, intentional conversations with it. Even if your anxiety is well managed, it helps to stay tuned in to it by having a good understanding of when, where, and how it typically shows up. When you do, you can almost predict the onset of anxiety and proactively intervene when it is in its early, more manageable stages.

For example, let's say you RSVP'd yes to a bridal shower scheduled in a couple of weeks. You know that your anxiety tends to show up in social situations in which you are required to mingle. You are pretty confident that you won't know many people at the shower and you will feel pressure to engage in small talk with strangers for some period of time. Your relationship with the bride is important to you, so you want to do your best to contribute to her having a good time.

The night before the event, your anxiety sets in. It is uncomfortable, so to drown it out, you feel the urge to have a few glasses of wine and binge a show on Netflix. As the night progresses, so does your anxiety, and you start having thoughts like *Tomorrow is going to be awful* and *I could just say that something has come up and I have to cancel.* These are examples of early nudges from anxiety that you should notice and tend to.

When you notice a nudge from anxiety, you have two choices: (1) Continue your efforts to extinguish your anxiety by numbing and avoiding and hope that works, or (2) acknowledge that your anxiety wants your attention and the only way to get it to chill is to spend some time with it. In the bridal shower example, your friendship with the bride is important to you, and you'd like to be there for her and take part with as little anxiety as possible, so the second option is the better choice. It might work like this:

1. You pause your show, put the wine down, and turn your attention inward. You say, *Okay, anxiety, what is it that you want?*

   Your anxiety tells you that it fears you are going to be super awkward and embarrass yourself.

2. You acknowledge that you too would like to avoid embarrassment at the shower. You thank your anxiety for alerting you to this. Now to come up with a plan with your anxiety for decreasing the likelihood that this will happen.

3. The plan: You make sure to take care of your basic needs first. You make a plan to get adequate sleep tonight, be sure to eat a good meal and avoid caffeine the next morning, and take a yoga class before you go to the shower. You then reach out to a mutual friend who confirms that she plans to attend the shower too. You make sure to get there early, sit near your mutual friend, and limit your mimosa intake to a maximum of two. You prepare a few conversation starters to use when the conversation gets awkward or stale, like "Have you seen the venue where Steph is getting married? It's so gorgeous!"

4. You feel good about this plan. Your anxiety breathes a sigh of relief. You feel slight relief from your anxiety.

Managing anxiety effectively requires awareness of when it is likely to show up and a willingness to respond to its nudges. The more information you have about when you can expect your anxiety to show up, the better you can predict and respond to it. When you know that you tend to get anxiety in social situations because you fear embarrassment, you can almost predict that it will show up the night before a social event. Because you have this knowledge, you can catch it early, when it is nudging you, and be proactive about how you're going to address it.

In addition to getting to know when your anxiety shows up, you should also have awareness of where and how it manifests. Maybe you know that you tend to get anxiety when you are in a crowded grocery store or a professional meeting. Perhaps your anxiety starts to nudge you when you go to a specific area of town or when you board an airplane.

Maybe it creeps in when you're at your family's house or at the doctor's office. When you have plans to go to a specific location where your anxiety is known to rise, you can check in with it beforehand and come up with a game plan together for navigating being in this place together.

REFLECTION: Getting to Know Your Anxiety— A Journal Exercise

Spend some time reflecting in your journal on the when, where, and hows of your anxiety. Get to know your anxiety's nudges versus its more urgent ways of communicating.

1. When is your anxiety most likely to show up? What is it trying to protect you from in these situations?

2. Where is your anxiety most likely to show up (meetings, airplanes, doctors' offices, and so on)? Do you know why this is? In other words, are these places connected to past little t traumas?

3. How does your anxiety usually manifest in your body? Do you typically become aware of body sensations first, or do these come later once your anxiety has progressed?

4. What are the first signs of a nudge from anxiety? What happens if you ignore these nudges?

5. What can you do when you experience the first signs of anxiety?

Step Two: Understanding Anxiety's Needs

The second step in building a healthy working relationship with your anxiety is to get clear on what your anxiety needs from you and to share with anxiety what you need from it. Just like in any relationship, this one is more likely to be successful if both partners have clear expectations of what they need in the relationship and have communicated those needs directly. Your relationship with anxiety is no different. It will take introspection, communication, and perhaps some negotiation to keep both parties happy and the relationship functioning well.

In chapter 5 you explored what anxiety needs from you while approaching past stuck memories. Now you are asked to gather more information about what your anxiety needs from you moving forward. Assume that experiencing anxiety in the future in inevitable. There will be future situations and places you encounter that will trigger your anxiety to alert you to something. It is likely that your anxiety will need you to be open to its concerns and to trust that what it has to say is important. It could be that your anxiety needs you to do your best to avoid situations or people who seem to pose a real threat to your well-being.

As in previous exercises, it is best to go inside and listen for information and answers from your anxiety rather than trying to figure out the answers with your logical mind. Approach the following exercise with a curious, open mind. (You can also find an audio version of this exercise to download in the online free tools at http://www.newharbinger.com /48756.)

EXERCISE: What Does Anxiety Need from You?

Find a place in your home or office that is free of distractions. In a comfortable seated position, close your eyes and turn your attention inward. Spend a few moments noticing, with an open mind, what is going on inside. Pay attention to your breath.

Now connect with the part of you that experiences anxiety. This part of you may show up right away, or perhaps it feels more distant and hard to reach. Don't try to force or make anything happen; just continue breathing with a curious, open perspective.

Once you are able to connect to the anxious part of you, find a place where you and your anxiety can have a conversation. Let it know that you're here to get to know what it needs from you from this point onward. Tell it that it is your goal to develop the best working relationship possible. If it feels right, share with it that you know it has an important role in keeping you safe, and you want to nourish your relationship with it as best as you can. Share with it what you've gathered about when, where, and how it shows up. Tell it that you're working hard to understand it.

Next, ask your anxiety if it wants to share any information with you about what it needs from you. Get quiet. Listen. It may give you an answer right away, or it may take more time to get this feedback. If you need clarity, ask your anxiety to tell you more. Tell it you would like as clear of information as possible, with all the detail it is willing to share.

Notice how you feel in response to what your anxiety has to say. Let go of any judgments or strong emotional reactions. Just observe. Listen. Now is not the time for arguing or negotiation; that can come later. Right now you are just gathering information. If necessary, take notes, as it's important to remember what your anxiety is telling you it needs moving forward.

Once you have a clear understanding of what it is saying, ask if there is anything else it needs. Let it continue to show you what it wants, while you remain curious and open. Once there is nothing more it needs to say, thank it for showing up today, and let it know you will take all that it has told you into consideration.

With this experience fresh in your mind, take out your journal and answer the following reflection questions.

1.   How accessible was your anxiety today? How difficult or easy was it to communicate with it?

2.   What did your anxiety communicate with you about what it needs from you?

3.   What are your reactions to what your anxiety had to say? Do you notice any feelings of resistance or pushback coming up for you?

4.   Are there any asks from your anxiety that you think you'll need to negotiate, or do they all seem fair and agreeable?

It could be that your anxiety made fairly simple requests, like *Listen to me* or *Don't push me away*. Or it could be that your anxiety had an overwhelming request that you're not sure if you can agree to, like *End that troubled relationship*. Ultimately, you are the one in control of your life. While it will benefit you to work with your anxiety on its requests, remember that anxiety often does not have all of the information that you do. It may take some time to process anxiety's requests and get clear on what you're willing to agree to versus what you aren't.

It is possible that you will need to negotiate some of anxiety's requests. For example, if anxiety made a request like *Don't go to any more social gatherings* and this is a request you are unwilling to fulfill, you will want to politely let your anxiety know that you hear its request and aren't able or willing to do this. However, you can do your best to come up with a plan with your anxiety to help it feel as safe and soothed as possible when these situations arise.

You may go inside and tell your anxiety something like, *I hear that you want me to stop going to social gatherings altogether. I know that these are uncomfortable and feel dangerous to you; however, they aren't actually dangerous, and there are times when attending a gathering is really important. When this happens, I will make sure to check in with you beforehand and come up with a game plan for making this as tolerable as possible for both of us.* Just like in any relationship, expression of needs from either party may require negotiation and meeting in the middle.

Step Three: Communicating Your Needs

Now that you have taken the time to hear what your anxiety needs from you, it is your turn to share with your anxiety what you need from it. Keep in mind that complete eradication of anxiety is not possible. Therefore, it is not in either of your best interests to ask it to go away completely. Think about what needs to happen so that you can experience anxiety while still living a values-driven life. Perhaps you need it to be willing to comply when you ask it to ease up somewhat on the feelings it triggers in you. Maybe you would like it to give you more clear nudges when it is trying to get your attention, as opposed to subtle ones that are followed by coming on suddenly and hard. You might want it to let you take the reins when navigating your intimate relationship so that anxiety does not sabotage it.

Spend some time reflecting on how you can cohabitate with anxiety effectively. If you imagine yourself a year from now living a life consistent with your values, with anxiety fairly well managed, what does that look like for you? How is that scenario different from the way you experience anxiety now?

Answer the following reflection questions in your journal.

- What do you need from anxiety as you navigate life moving forward?

- How you do envision living a fulfilled, meaningful life while still having some anxiety?

Once you have an idea of what you need from anxiety, you will need to communicate your needs with it. It is not enough to just think about what you need; for this to stick, you need to tell your anxiety and get its acknowledgment and feedback. In the following exercise, share with anxiety what you need from it. (You can also find an audio version of this exercise to download in the online free tools at http://www.newhar binger.com/48756.)

EXERCISE: Share Your Needs with Anxiety

Find a place in your home or office that is free of distractions. In a comfortable seated position or reclining, close your eyes and turn your attention inward. Without judgment, start by noticing what is going on inside. Pay attention to your breath.

Now see if you can connect with the part of you that experiences anxiety. This part of you may show up right away, or perhaps it feels more distant and hard to reach. Don't try to force or make anything happen; just continue breathing with a curious, open perspective.

Once you are able to connect to the anxious part of you, invite your anxiety to a meeting place where you can have a conversation. Let it know that you appreciated it sharing its needs with you, and now you are going to do the same. Tell it that your goal is to establish great communication with it. When you have its attention, gently let anxiety know what you need from it. Ask it to just listen for now until you are finished. If any negotiation is necessary, that can happen later. Try to communicate with your anxiety in a compassionate, warm voice. Be specific and clear.

When you are finished communicating what you need from your anxiety, let it know that you are open to feedback. Ask it directly if it is willing to agree to your requests. Notice the energy in the room between you and your anxiety. Is it open and safe? If not, what needs to happen to make it more so? Take breathers as necessary. Take turns respectfully sharing your thoughts until it feels like you have come to an agreement. This may take more than one conversation.

With the experience fresh in your mind, reflect in your journal on the following questions :

1. What requests did you make to your anxiety?

2. What was your anxiety's response? Did it agree to your requests?

3. Are there any needs that will require future discussion or negotiation?

4. Are there any additional needs you want to communicate to anxiety but haven't yet?

Step Four: Negotiation

Just as in any relationship, good communication with your anxiety requires an ongoing effort from both parties. It is not typical that you can have one conversation in which you assert a need of yours and it is then met perfectly forever after. Even if you clearly communicated your needs and the other party acknowledged and agreed to them, it is likely you'll need to revisit the conversation at some point in the future. Additionally, it may take multiple conversations until you feel like your need was truly acknowledged and agreed to.

For example, if you asked your anxiety to loosen its grip in your relationship, it could be that your anxiety was skeptical, as it fears what might happen if you let your guard down. Negotiating this could require lots of dialogue over the course of several conversations. Remember that anxiety has been reinforced over and over again through time and will need some practice to loosen its grip. Perhaps you have gone inside and told anxiety that you would like it to stop sabotaging relationships at the first sight of conflict. Maybe you helped it understand that conflict in relationships can actually mean your (human) partner wants to preserve the relationship, not abandon you. In your initial conversation, anxiety seems to grasp this concept and agrees to ease up the next time you disagree with your partner. A few months go by, and things are great, and then out of nowhere your partner sends you a text saying that something has been bothering him and he'd like to talk to you about it later. Your anxiety spikes. It continues to escalate throughout the day, despite your conversation with it months ago. When this happens, you will need to have another conversation with it.

If you sense that your need(s) requires some negotiation with your anxiety, consider the following questions to ask anxiety to propel the discussion forward:

- What do you need in order to trust that it is safe for you to ease up?

- What can I do to help you not have to work so hard?

- If you agree to ease up, what signal will you give to me if you need to get my attention?

- How can I help you trust that I hear your concerns and will take them seriously?

- Are you willing to do an experiment in which you ease up for a short period of time and see how I do?

After you and your anxiety come to an agreement on how to move forward together, you will want to have follow-up conversations in which you may renegotiate your needs. For example, let's say you ask your anxiety to ease up in your relationship so that you don't inadvertently sabotage it. Anxiety agrees, and it begins to trust that you can navigate relationships without its constant input. Then your partner unexpectedly breaks up with you. It is possible that your anxiety will want to swoop in and take back control, believing that you were hurt solely because it had become less vigilant. Your anxiety does not have all of the information that you have, and it may become more rigid in its perspective on what it needs from you in relationships and vice versa. If this happens, you'll need to renegotiate.

In this example, you would want to go inside and allow anxiety to share its thoughts and feelings about what happened. Then you would share yours. You might help anxiety understand that despite the relationship's ending, it was one of the most fulfilling ones you've had because you were willing to be vulnerable. You might think of all of the growth you had in this relationship, and how it will make you better equipped for the next relationship. You might ask your anxiety to continue trusting you, despite the relationship's ending. You might help it understand that the end of a relationship isn't actually always the worst thing. You also might help it to see that the ending of the relationship wouldn't necessarily be less painful if you had been hypervigilant throughout its duration.

Revisiting Trauma

There may be times when it feels like you get stuck when trying to come to an agreement with your anxiety. This may be one indicator that there is a past little t trauma that must be addressed before any future working relationship can be established. If, for example, your anxiety will not budge in your request that it ease up in your relationship, it could be an indicator that a little t trauma in your past remains as a boulder to which you are tethered, keeping you stuck. In that case, you may need to revisit chapters 5 and 6 to help you become unstuck from that event and then revisit your communication plan with anxiety from here on out.

It could also be that you need to revisit a past memory that you had already addressed and thought was processed. This does not mean that your initial work was ineffective or that you have lost any progress. It simply means that you need to revisit a topic with your anxiety, much as you might revisit the same conversation with your intimate partner despite thinking it had previously been resolved. This work is not linear; indeed, it can feel like two steps forward, one step back. (This is normal— and we'll explore this truth further in the next chapter.) You will know you need to revisit a past memory when it feels like your anxiety is stuck in trauma time, does not fit the facts of the current situation, and/or is showing up frequently and not responding well to logic and reasoning.

You may be thinking, *This sounds like a lot of work!*—and if you are, you are correct. But it is also a lot of work to live with anxiety in the driver's seat of your life. All healthy relationships take effort, and if you want a healthy relationship with your anxiety, the effort required is no different. You likely have certain people in your life whom you value enough that you are willing to put in the work to keep the relationship healthy and functioning well. My hope is that you see the value in putting in the work to keep your relationship with your anxiety healthy and well-balanced. After all, your relationship with anxiety may be the one relationship in your life that has the power to influence all the others.

In the next chapter, we'll delve into how to manage future anxiety setbacks (which are inevitable) without becoming discouraged; we'll also consider how to deal with anxiety about not having anxiety. We'll explore the job that you'd like anxiety to do now that it will no longer be alerting you to danger that doesn't actually exist. Now that you will be less consumed by anxiety, what do you actually want to do with your time? What kind of person do you want to be? To start discovering these possibilities, together we'll explore your values.

CHAPTER 8

beyond the boulders

At this point, you have been offered a new way to think about anxiety, opportunities to repair your relationship with anxiety, avenues for uncovering and processing the root of your anxiety, and strategies for building a working relationship with your anxiety for the future. While it was necessary to present these steps in a linear, orderly way for the flow of this book, healing from anxiety is not typically linear, and it is never one-and-done.

When you sprain your ankle, you are almost guaranteed complete healing in a few weeks if you follow the instructions of your doctor. Once your ankle has healed, you will be able to put the injury behind you and will not need to continue to tend to it. Anxiety does not work this way, because it is not an injury; it does not need to be fixed or remedied. It is an adaptive emotion that, when working correctly, helps you avoid danger and live meaningfully. You'll need to continue understanding and collaborating with your anxiety if it is to continue helping you live a fulfilled life consistent with your values.

Anxiety Relapses

I hope that by this point in the work you are feeling like you have made some progress in understanding and working with your anxiety. Perhaps your anxiety has become more distant, like a quiet observer rather than a force to be reckoned with. With the work you have been doing, it may even seem as if anxiety has completely gone away for now, and you feel more clear headed and calm. Regardless of the progress you have made thus far, it is highly likely that you will experience times in the future in which anxiety still gets the best of you.

For example, you might have done some good work on social anxiety and experienced improvement in your ability to engage in groups with more spontaneity and ease. You may feel like social anxiety is a thing of the past. Then all of a sudden one day you are getting ready to go to a small gathering at a friend's house and you experience a panic attack, seemingly out of nowhere. If you've felt like you were past this by now, this can be highly discouraging. The thought that you have regressed and lost your progress can be seriously depressing.

When this happens, it is useful to pay attention to primary versus secondary emotions. Primary emotions are emotions that come first. Secondary emotions are emotions that we have *about* primary emotions. Secondary emotions tend to complicate things and prolong our pain. For example, if you have a panic attack before a gathering at a friend's house, fear may be the primary emotion. It sets in, peaks, and then is over, usually within a few minutes. Following the wave of fear and panic, you experience frustration because you start thinking that maybe you didn't make the progress you thought you had made. You might also be discouraged because you think nothing is ever going to work for you and you will have to live with panic attacks forever. Then hopelessness and depression set in, and you cancel your plans to attend the gathering.

In this example, fear was the primary emotion, which then elicited a panic response. It lasted just a few minutes. Then came the secondary emotions about the panic—frustration, discouragement, hopelessness, and depression. In this case the secondary emotions—the emotions about your primary emotion—cause more distress and suffering than the primary emotion you initially experienced.

When you have what feels like an anxiety relapse, acknowledging and releasing your secondary emotions can keep you on the path toward healing. To do this, you might repeat thoughts like *The healing journey is not linear* or *This was a minor setback* or *Two steps forward, one step back* or *This does not erase my progress.* Once you have worked through and released your secondary emotions, you clear up space in your mind to gather more information about what led up to the primary emotion. Then you can go inside, initiate a conversation with your anxiety, and explore the factors that contributed to its sounding the alarm. Gaining this new information and insight becomes the next step forward on your healing journey.

Once you understand the probability that you will succumb to anxiety at some point in the future, you'll feel less taken by surprise when it happens, and you'll be better able to keep secondary emotions at bay. Anxiety relapses can happen for a multitude of reasons that have nothing to do with the progress you have already made. An unexpected big wave of anxiety is usually the result of an accumulation of lots of smaller factors. When you get curious and explore what led up to the anxiety relapse, you may find the basis for it: perhaps you are running on very little sleep, or dealing with the stress of a new job or a move, or taking a new medication that is affecting your brain chemistry. Or perhaps a new little t trauma has been activated.

When you have an anxiety relapse, it can be useful to journal about the thoughts, feelings, and body sensations you had leading up to the anxiety spike, during the spike, and afterward. When you start to examine the internal and external factors present before the spike, you will get good information about what contributed to your anxiety. Take the example of my client who had a panic attack while in the parking lot. When she first described the event to me, she said she panicked "out of nowhere." After exploring it further, we identified several potential triggers: a fight with her husband, having not eaten lunch that day, and a recent change to her medications. Once she had this context, she was able to adopt some self-compassion and see that her anxiety had not come out of nowhere after all.

Regardless of what led up to the setback, it's important to do the reflecting work early so that you can get back on track quickly. Don't allow an anxiety setback to convince you that this work is futile and you should give up now. Take the time you need to process what happened, let your secondary emotions subside, and get curious and open about what your anxiety needs to share with you. Then take this information and get back out there in the world. Go to the next gathering.

Anxiety About Not Having Anxiety

In addition to anxiety spikes or setbacks, you may have times when your anxiety feels very well managed. You could even experience times when it feels nonexistent. When this happens, I imagine your primary emotion is relief or contentment. After all, you have invested a lot of time and energy into making it this far. But then, if you are like many people prone to anxiety, something curious may happen: you may start to experience being *anxious about not being anxious*. You feel like you must not get too comfortable, because something terrible could be around the corner. You are concerned about being caught off guard, and you don't yet trust that things could just be okay. Feeling calm feels good, but ominous—it's like you're waiting for the other shoe to drop.

This is an indicator that your anxiety is trying to alert you to the danger associated with thinking things are okay or feeling calm. While this might make your head spin, because it feels so ridiculous, it actually is no different from any other function of anxiety. It could be that there is a little t trauma associated with being caught off guard that needs to be addressed. Was there an earlier time when you felt calm and then something bad happened? Was there a time when you thought things were okay and then you were blindsided? Where, when, and how did you learn that feeling calm is not safe? You may find it helpful to go back there and work through it, as you already did with other little t traumas.

The other possibility when experiencing anxiety about not having anxiety is that your anxiety is not used to being idle, and it isn't sure what else to do. In other words, your anxiety needs another job to occupy it. All parts of ourselves have an important job description; they have gotten quite good at their jobs and probably take pride in them. Doing this work creates changes to anxiety's job description. You are essentially removing items from its job description when you show it that it doesn't need to alert you to looming events like social gatherings and public speaking, or concerns like the expected *not* happening; say, when your partner still hasn't texted you back and it's been a good half hour! (Well, a good fifteen minutes.)

Think about how you would feel in the unlikely event that your boss told you they'd eliminated 80 percent of your job description. You might initially feel relieved, thinking *Finally this job will feel manageable!* Then it's likely you'd start to twiddle your thumbs and wonder what you're supposed to do with all that extra time. Over time, you might feel bored and seek out other things to do. This is what your anxiety is experiencing when you cut back its workload. Anxiety is high achieving—it wants a job to do!

It can be useful to explore with your anxiety what it would like to do instead of alert you to danger all of the time. Then you can renegotiate its job description in a way that honors your preference for it to relax on the tasks it used to do, while replacing those things with other tasks that it finds meaningful. The following exercise guides you through this process.

EXERCISE: Exploring Anxiety's New Job

Find a place in your home or office that is free of distractions. In a comfortable seated position or reclining, close your eyes and turn your attention inward. Spend a few moments with openness and curiosity about what is going on inside. Pay attention to your breath.

Now connect with the part of you that experiences anxiety. This part of you may show up right away, or perhaps it feels more distant right now. Don't try to force or make anything happen; just continue breathing with a curious, open perspective.

Once you are able to connect to the anxious part of you, find a place inside where you and your anxiety can have a conversation. Let it know that you're here to get to know what it needs from you now. Tell your anxiety that you can see the effort it is making to ease up some. Ask your anxiety: *Now that you no longer need to work as hard at alerting me to danger, what would you like to do instead?*

Before you start making suggestions, let anxiety tell you what it would like to do. If it is stumped, offer some alternative jobs you can think of. Perhaps it wants to work on some other important task. Maybe it wants to play or create. Maybe it is fine with just resting for now. Come to a mutual agreement. Shake on it if you'd like. Reassure your anxiety that this new role comes with more fulfillment, fun, and payoff for everyone. It is a promotion. Invite anxiety to assume its new role, and agree to check in with it in a week or two to see how it feels about its new job. Reassure your anxiety that you can always make modifications to its job description as needed.

A client I worked with had anxiety about people leaving her. This interfered with her ability to make and maintain healthy friendships, because she worried that people would just leave. She traced this fear back to a big T trauma of her dad leaving her family when she was little. We revisited this memory together, and in the course of therapy, she relieved her four-year-old inner child of the responsibility for her dad's leaving. She exclaimed, "It was not my job to make sure he stayed around."

Once her inner child no longer needed to alert her to threats of abandonment in her current friendships, she wondered what to do instead. Rather than make suggestions to my client or her inner child directly, I invited my client to go inside and ask her inner child what she would like to do. To her surprise, her inner child responded quickly and confidently that she wanted to have fun playing with dolls instead. We agreed on the new job, and since then, her anxiety about being abandoned in friendships has been nearly extinguished.

Waning Motivation for This Work

You may find that your motivation to do this work waxes and wanes over time. This is a natural, expected part of the process of healing. When you get this far in the book and the work, you'll likely still feel at least somewhat motivated to work on your anxiety. But once you finish the book and more and more time passes in which you are not actively engaging in this work, you may find your motivation to stay in touch with your anxiety drops off. You can't be expected to maintain 100-percent motivation for all things self-improvement all of the time. That sounds a lot like missing out on the fun stuff life has to offer.

While declining motivation is to be expected, it is also something to be mindful of, because it can mean you slip back into old habits of trying to work against your anxiety. I hope that the methods you have learned here will give you a new way of looking at your anxiety that you will keep with you forever, so that running away from your anxiety will not be your default response. It's human nature to avoid things that cause us discomfort, so your natural impulse, without a concerted effort to do otherwise, will be to avoid or extinguish anxiety. You'll need some motivation to maintain a working relationship with your anxiety.

A big part of maintaining this motivation is to assess and reassess your values—the things you care about at the most fundamental level. Values are different from goals. Goals are achievements that can be checked off on a to-do list, like graduating from college, getting a job, or saving money for a trip. Values are how you want to live your life and be remembered. You can't ever "achieve" them; they require ongoing effort. Values are a way of being rather than doing.

When helping my clients explore their values, I like to ask these two questions:

- If you were to die tomorrow and the people you love most were gathered at your funeral, reminiscing about the kind of person you were, what would you want them to say about you?

- If you knew you had twenty-four hours left to live, what would you do with that time? Where would you go? With whom would you spend it? What would you say?

When asked about her values, one of my clients recently reported that she wanted to be remembered as helpful and funny. She quickly made the connection that unmanaged anxiety was a hindrance to being both of those things. Her anxiety often caused her to be a recluse—canceling plans with friends and shutting out the world around her. The reflection on her values was an important reminder to her of her *why* for doing this work. It is not to live with less discomfort; rather, it is to live more fully.

Spend some time considering how you might answer these questions, then reflect in your journal.

- How do you want to be remembered when you are no longer here?

- What would you do with just twenty-four hours left to live on this earth?

- What did you learn from your reflections about what you value most?

If you are unsure about your answers, consider the following list of possible values and how those might be reflected in those remembrances of you, and in your wishes for that final day:

Kindness

Generosity

Honesty

Adventure

Fun

Creativity

Service to Others

Humor

Loyalty

Strength

Friendship

Courage

Helpfulness

Spirituality

Compassion

Your values are your why for doing the work you're doing in this book. Once you have identified your most fundamental values, you might start to see how anxiety gets in the way of carrying them out. Untreated anxiety likely pulls you further away from your values. It can convince you that you should avoid taking risks or being spontaneous or adventurous. It can also get in the way of being a reliable friend, a helpful neighbor, or a compassionate partner.

When you participate in life despite your anxiety, you are more easily able to live a life consistent with your values. When you are in tune with your values, you may experience a newfound motivation to do the work to keep your anxiety well managed. Engaging in the inner reflection conversations with your anxiety, as you've been doing here, is not just about having conversations with anxiety. You're not revisiting the origins of your anxiety just to see where it came from. And as you practice the exposures necessary to confront rather than avoid anxiety, you're not just challenging yourself for no good reason. You're working to live a life that is meaningful to you—to act right now in accordance with how you want to be remembered when you are gone. It's the difference between existing and living fully.

One of my former clients had anxiety about leaving the house. Her anxiety started as much more specific, but had progressed and generalized over time. Once she was informed she would have to return to work in person after the COVID-19 pandemic, she knew she needed to seek therapy. Together we created a list of exposures, which included leaving the house to go for a five-minute walk, then driving to her local Target store, followed by driving to a shopping mall in the nearest town over and spending a couple of hours there. Some anxiety setbacks made her question whether the therapeutic work was worth the effort. She felt waning motivation to keep doing the exposure homework I assigned her between sessions.

As a way to tap into more motivation, I asked her how she would like to spend her last twenty-four hours on this earth. I wanted to know what she valued. With tears in her eyes, she told me this beautiful story.

She used to host annual crawfish boils in her neighborhood. She would invite all of her friends and family, and people would even fly in from out of town to attend. People brought their kids from all over; they would come together and play in the neighborhood. There was laughter, games, and good food. Everyone would stay up late into the night, cele-brating nothing but life itself. But because of my client's anxiety, she hadn't been able to host or attend a crawfish boil in years. People had been asking her when she would host again. She usually responded by saying she wasn't sure. She wasn't comfortable telling people that she didn't know when her anxiety would ease up enough to allow her to.

Hearing this story showed me that she valued family, friendship, connection, fun, and laughter. Once we uncovered these values, the homework I assigned her served a completely different purpose. When I asked her to leave her house to go shopping outside of town despite the anxiety it would cause, it wasn't for the sake of being able to purchase goods that weren't available in her town. In fact, that was hardly a moti-vator. Doing this work, getting anxiety under control, would bring her closer, step by step, to being able to host another crawfish boil. That became her why.

Considering your values will help you discover your why for doing this work. It is usually deeper than wanting to not feel so anxious. You already know that you can tolerate anxiety. You have been coexisting with it for some time now. If you just wanted tools for managing anxiety, you could have stopped reading this book after chapter 2. This work isn't about wrangling anxiety.

Think about all the reasons that made you buy this book. You are not doing this work to eradicate symptoms. You are doing it for the doors that will open in your life when your anxiety loosens its grip. This work is about being able to say yes to attending social gatherings and having a blast at them. It is about showing up authentically and unapologetically in new relationships without hiding parts of yourself. It is about taking spontaneous trips. It is about dancing the night away. It is about taking risks and maybe making some bad decisions. It is about courage. It is about your inner child being proud of the life you are living. It is about hosting that crawfish boil.

The work it takes to repair your relationship with anxiety is no easy feat. You have made it this far, and you should be proud of the effort you have put in to better yourself and improve your relationships. It is much easier to maintain the status quo than it is to face your anxiety—and the memories that caused and reinforced it over time—head on. It takes serious courage to be willing to walk into your past experiences and poke around at what hurts. Just as your brain and body would not like you to rip off a bandage and start poking at a wound on your arm, it is counterintuitive to explore the wounds that led to your anxiety in this way. To do so means you are courageous and committed to living a life with purpose and meaning. Regardless of the outcome of this work for you, your effort is something to be celebrated.

If, as you near the end of this book, you have the thought, *Darn it! I've finished the book and I still have anxiety!*—please know that you are not alone. Never in my therapy practice have I had a client come to their last therapy session and say, "That's it! I am healed. I no longer have any anxiety, and I'm ready to end therapy!" More commonly, termination from therapy happens after a series of conversations about what realistic growth looks like, how the person might start to incorporate newfound tools learned in therapy into their day-to-day life as they move forward without therapy, and the option to return to therapy in the future when extra support is needed. The same is true for you with this work. The bad news: You probably won't ever arrive at the destination of Healed— because it doesn't exist. The good news: Nobody arrives there, so you don't have to either. This work is an unfolding journey that can and should be returned to as needed. It is a process rather than a milestone.

Committing to self-improvement is commendable. At the same time, you are not a constant self-improvement project. Perfectionism has no place in this work (or anywhere)—it can only lead to feelings of inadequacy. To be human is to experience emotions, including the uncomfortable, messy ones. Even with crippling anxiety, you are worthy of love, acceptance, and belonging.

Perhaps you are experiencing newfound ease, calm, and confidence as a result of doing this work. Perhaps it has also stirred up some conflicting or confusing feelings within you. You might feel like you still have a lot to learn about your anxiety. Regardless of how much progress you feel you have made, or how much more you think you still need to make, remember to have grace with yourself. You can be simultaneously working to better yourself and knowing that you are already enough. You are inherently whole.

I hope that this book has brought you closer to yourself. I hope it has shown you that you are to be trusted. With *you* by your side, you can climb the mountain of life without restriction. You are simultaneously free—and home.

References

Anderson, F., PhD. 2020, April 22. "Treating Complex Trauma with Internal Family Systems." Lecture presented via PESI, Inc. in Phoenix, AZ.

Martin, K. M. 2012. "How to Use Fraser's Dissociative Table Technique to Access and Work with Emotional Parts of the Personality." *Journal of EMDR Practice and Research* 6(4): 179–186. https://connect.springerpub.com/content/sgremdr/6/4/179.

Levine, P. A., PhD. n.d. Somatic Experiencing (SE). Retrieved November 8, 2020, from https://www.somaticexperiencing.com/somatic-experiencing.

Shapiro, F. 1995. *Eye Movement Desensitization and Reprocessing: Basic Principles, Protocols, and Procedures.* New York, NY: Guilford Press.

Shapiro, F. 2001. *Eye Movement Desensitization and Reprocessing: Basic Principles, Protocols, and Procedures.* 2nd ed. New York, NY: Guilford Press.

Shapiro, F. 2012. *Getting Past Your Past: Take Control of Your Life with Self-Help Techniques from EMDR Therapy.* Emmaus, PA: Rodale.

Siegel, D. J. 1999. *The Developing Mind: How Relationships and the Brain Interact to Shape Who We Are.* New York, NY: Guilford Press.

Solomon, R. M., and F. Shapiro. 2008. "EMDR and the Adaptive Information Processing Model: Potential Mechanisms of Change." *Journal of EMDR Practice and Research* 2(4): 315–325.

Stinson, A. n.d. "Adult-Onset Asthma: Causes, Symptoms, Treatments, and Management." *Medical News Today.* https://www.medicalnewstoday.com/articles/325302.

Jaime Castillo, LCSW, is founder of Find Your Shine Therapy, and a licensed clinical social worker specializing in the treatment of trauma and anxiety disorders. She is a certified eye movement desensitization and reprocessing (EMDR) therapist and EMDRIA-approved consultant, and has additional training in internal family systems (IFS) and exposure therapy. She specializes in working with adults experiencing post-traumatic stress disorder (PTSD), obsessive-compulsive disorder (OCD), phobias, and generalized anxiety disorder (GAD). Jaime has been featured for her trauma expertise in *The Arizona Republic*, *The Verge*, and *Phoenix Voyage Magazine* where she was named a Top Inspiring Phoenix Professional. She was a speaker at the 2020 Global Resiliency Summit alongside world-renowned mental health professionals, and appeared as a guest trauma and shame expert on *The Things We Couldn't Say* podcast.

Real change *is* possible

For more than forty-five years, New Harbinger has published proven-effective self-help books and pioneering workbooks to help readers of all ages and backgrounds improve mental health and well-being, and achieve lasting personal growth. In addition, our spirituality books offer profound guidance for deepening awareness and cultivating healing, self-discovery, and fulfillment.

Founded by psychologist Matthew McKay and Patrick Fanning, New Harbinger is proud to be an independent, employee-owned company. Our books reflect our core values of integrity, innovation, commitment, sustainability, compassion, and trust. Written by leaders in the field and recommended by therapists worldwide, New Harbinger books are practical, accessible, and provide real tools for real change.

newharbingerpublications

MORE BOOKS from
NEW HARBINGER PUBLICATIONS

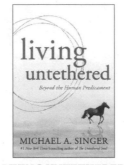

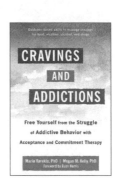